TIN CAN COOK

JACK MONROE
TIN CAN COOK

bluebird
books for life

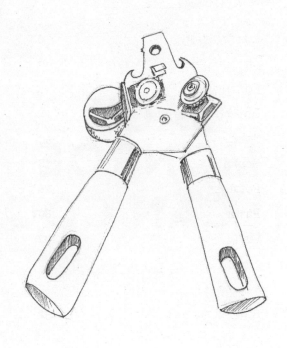

CONTENTS

INTRODUCTION

WELCOME TO **TIN CAN COOK**

This is my fourth cookbook, and I've seen inside enough kitchen cupboards by now to be fascinated by our relationship with tinned foods, and what those tins can say about us. Our abilities, our fears, our emergencies, our comfort zones. Tins with ring pulls attached tend to belong to those with slightly more disposable income; look carefully at the Basics and Value ranges next time you're in the supermarket and you'll see that they require a tin opener to get into them. The irony, that those with the least money need an additional piece of kitchen equipment in order to eat the most basic food stuffs.

Foodbanks – once a quaint Dickensian idea of a 'big society', now sit squarely in every community in the United Kingdom. At the time of writing this, there are around four hundred, providing 1.5 million food parcels a year to people who would be at risk of starving without them, and those parcels are made up primarily of tins. I know, because I was a foodbank user for six long months. It was out of those parcels that I started to write my early recipes online, mostly for something to do, and then as my blog grew in popularity, out of a sense of duty and necessity.

I have gone on to write 'cold box recipes', for people who are homeless or have no access to kitchens. 'Kettle recipes' for people who – you guessed it – have only a kettle to heat their food. And recipes from tin cans for charity dinners, for foodbank users, for a pop-up restaurant to raise awareness of an 'Eat Or Heat' campaign, and for my books.

The late, former BBC cook Shirley Goode once wrote about my first book, *A Girl Called Jack*, that 'cooking with yoghurt and a jar of fish paste doesn't take any particular skill'. In my *Guardian* recipe column, readers would tut below the lines in the comments section every time I chopped a tin of potatoes into a saag aloo or casserole, so I responded by including an entire chapter of the blessed bleached things in *Cooking on a Bootstrap* by way of retort. I have spent years rinsing the sticky orange sauce from 23p baked beans to reveal the runty little haricots beneath, at a third of the price of the plain ones – a great alternative if you can handle the slightly luminescent tinge that doesn't quite come off.

We have an odd culinary relationship with tinned food. In higher society, rare and supposedly exquisite goods like tinned baby octopus, foie gras and caviar come in beautifully crafted, artistically designed tins. They are collectors' items; one former friend kept a display of every tin of caviar she had ever eaten, an understated trophy cabinet of excess and moral turpitude. The restaurant Tincan, designed by the Tate, popped up briefly in Soho, in London, with hundreds of tins of expensive fish lining the walls to be selected by the customer and served with a chunk of bread, a pinch of salt and an eye-watering bill.

At the other end of the spectrum, I fill my shopping trolley with identical white labelled tins, the contents scrawled on the front as though in a child's hand, with no ring pull on the top, and barely a clue to their contents. At 20p, carrots in a tin are cheaper than fresh. Tinned tomatoes contain more lycopene, a cancer-fighting agent, than their fresh counterparts. Tinned potatoes can be up to a sixth of the price of even the cheapest fresh varieties. Sweetcorn, mushy peas, beans and lentils are all basic staples that can be thrown together into a variety of surprising meals. Tinned sardines contain almost an entire day's recommended intake of vitamins D and B12. The Tin Can Cook is one who can open their cupboard and create a meal from its contents on any given day, whatever they may be.

As I said, it's an odd relationship that we have with tinned goods. But we all have them, lurking in our kitchens, and I'm here to show you how you can create beautiful, delicious and nourishing meals by simply chucking a few of them together.

These recipes are designed for everyone – from those with very little cooking confidence and ability, the smallest of kitchens and the scantest of equipment, all the way up the culinary spectrum to the gourmands, the bon vivants, the entertainers, the practical jokers among us. I once cooked a three-course meal for a group of diners at a five-star hotel entirely from the cheapest tins in the supermarket. They loved the food, but their reactions when we did the 'big reveal' and showed them that it all came from a pile of tin cans, was absolutely priceless. Most laughed, some were embarrassed, one man was memorably apoplectic. Oh, I laughed at his furious notion that somehow tinned potatoes were going to kill him, when moments before he had declared it the best meal he had ever eaten. You can, of course, recreate these recipes with fresh ingredients if you like, but where's the fun in that? Grab your tin opener, and an open mind, and come with me.

SHOPPING NOTES

For the purposes of simplicity, and in order to make this cookbook accessible to people with a range of abilities, I have chosen to use the simpler option, where available, for each ingredient. More experienced cooks may find it slightly frustrating to have to reverse-engineer the recipe lists if choosing to use, say, garlic bulbs in place of garlic paste, but few food writers cater to newcomers, and so I must try. If you are a more confident cook, you'll know how much liquid stock comes from a cube (around 450ml), how many onions 100g of frozen onion represents (a small one) and how to make your own pease pudding (why bother?).

As a novice cook I found myself put off by overtly flouncy language and unfamiliar terminology, and my readers tell me the same. So, I hope you take these recipes in the spirit that they are intended; as a beginner's guide to cooking with tinned and pre-prepared ingredients, rather than anything that will ever compete for Michelin stars or similar.

For the new cook, as your confidence grows in the kitchen, I hope you will stray from these recipes, add your own twists to them, venture into fresh ingredients if you want to, even make your own garlic pastes, pestos and similar. Learning to cook is like most of us learning to walk; the first few attempts will be clumsy, futile, perhaps even a little painful – and frustrating – but if you keep getting up and having a crack at it, one day you'll barely even remember not being able to do it. You just need to take the first step.

CANSPLAINING: CAN TINNED FOOD BE GOOD FOR ME?

I knew as soon as I pitched the idea for this book that I would be deluged by critics keen to share their perceived wisdom about how 'canned food isn't good for you'. I've had this throughout my career as a food writer – from comments on my *Guardian* recipes, to emails, to a handwritten letter on fancy notepaper instructing me that I was a 'dangerous woman' for using tinned potatoes. Here is my retort to the cansplainers, once and for all; an A to Z of tinned goods, and how good they really are. I've tried not to go too heavy on the science, and I hope it makes for interesting reading.

A detailed study by the University of California found that:

'… Freezing and canning processes may preserve nutrient value. The initial thermal treatment of processed products can cause loss of water-soluble and oxygen-labile nutrients such as vitamin C and the B vitamins. However, these nutrients are relatively stable during subsequent canned storage owing to the lack of oxygen. Frozen products lose fewer nutrients initially because of the short heating time in blanching … exclusive recommendations of fresh produce ignore the nutrient benefits of canned and frozen products.

Many fresh fruits and vegetables have a shelf life of only days before they are unsafe or undesirable for consumption. Storage and processing technologies have been utilized for centuries to transform these perishable fruits and vegetables into safe, delicious and stable products. Refrigeration slows down the respiration of fruits and vegetables and allows for longer shelf lives. Freezing, canning and drying all serve to transform perishable fruits and vegetables into products that can be consumed year round and transported safely to consumers all over the world, not only those located near the growing region.'[1]

In short, although canning can cause a slight loss of some nutrients, notably vitamin C in some fruits and vegetables when heat-treated, the nutrient value once canned remains stable. And nutrients from canned and frozen fruits and vegetables are arguably more desirable than none at all.

There is some consternation about the potential presence of bisphenol A (BPA) – a plastic coating chemical – used in the lining of some tins. BPA can theoretically interact with oestrogen receptors in the body. The US Food and Drug Administration states that 'normal levels of canned food consumption have no adverse effects on general health', and as of 2016, major manufacturers have pledged to remove the BPA lining from their tins. I mention it merely as a precaution – and because it would be remiss of me to overlook it – but not to cause alarm.

CANSPLAINING AT-A-GLANCE

Anchovies The majority of fats in anchovies are the healthy variety – from omega-3 fatty acids. One serving contains more than 20 per cent of an adult's recommended daily intake of vitamin B3, and they are also a good source of selenium and protein.

Artichokes The artichoke is one of the oldest remedial plants, with records of its use as a medicine dating back to 400 BCE. Ancient Greeks and Romans used the artichoke for digestive problems, and in the 16th century, artichokes were documented as a treatment for liver problems and jaundice. Artichokes are low in saturated fat, and very low in cholesterol. They are also a source of magnesium, dietary fibre, vitamins C, K and vitamin B9.

Asparagus This is a source of vitamins A, C, E, K as well as vitamin B9, iron and fibre.

Baked beans Look out for the low-salt and low-sugar versions of these, although in recent times manufacturers have been far more cautious about making healthy versions of 'fast' foods. Baked beans are a source of magnesium, phosphorous, potassium, zinc and copper. In some of my recipes I rinse off the sticky orange sauce and use them as small white beans, in others I'm happy to just sling the whole lot in, sauce and all.

Beef (stewed steak) Beef is a good source of protein – even beef that comes in a can! You can also grab yourself some vitamin B12, zinc, selenium, iron, vitamin B3 and vitamin B6 here.

Berries In addition to containing antioxidants, many also contain considerable amounts of vitamin C.

Black beans These beans are a staple food in Central and South America. A great source of fibre, protein and vitamin B9, they are also a good source of copper, manganese, vitamin B1, phosphorus, magnesium and iron.

Black-eyed beans These are a source of fibre, potassium, protein and iron.

Borlotti beans These are a source of calcium, iron, magnesium, phosphorous, potassium, zinc and copper.

Broad beans Also known as fava beans, broad beans contain no saturated fat or cholesterol, making them a healthy choice. They also contain potassium, copper, selenium, zinc and are a source of magnesium. They are also an inexpensive source of protein.

Butter beans Low in fat and a source of protein, butter beans contain zinc which helps to maintain a healthy immune system.

Cannellini beans A good source of carbohydrates and protein, cannellini beans contain several B vitamins, including B12. They also provide iron, potassium, zinc and other essential minerals.

Carrots Known for being a source of beta-carotene that is converted by the body to vitamin A, carrots are also a good source of vitamin K.

Cherries These are a good source of vitamin C: you can find up to 16 per cent of our suggested daily intake in half a standard tin (150g). Cherries also contain fibre. Half a tin provides a source of potassium – around 350mg – which plays a key role in muscle, heart, kidney and nerve cell functions.

Chickpeas Also known as garbanzo beans, chickpeas are a good source of protein, carbohydrates and fibre. The iron, phosphorous, calcium, magnesium, manganese, zinc and vitamin K in chickpeas all contribute to building and maintaining bone strength.

Chopped pork Although admittedly high in sodium, fat and calories, chopped pork products such as Spam also provide protein and several micronutrients, such as zinc, potassium, iron and copper. Not one for everyday consumption, but there's some goodness in there if you look hard enough.

Clams If you're lucky enough to find these at a low price you can sling them over pasta, or into a soup or chowder. They are a good source of zinc, protein and omega-3 fatty acids, as well as a source of potassium, manganese and phosphorous.

Cockles A seaside favourite, cockles also come in tins and can be found at most supermarkets. They are a good source of vitamin B12, iron, iodine, selenium, omega-3 fatty acids and phosphorous.

Coconut milk Containing a mixture of saturated and non-saturated fats, coconut milk is a good source of potassium. Use it in curries, as a base for soups, or for baking in luxurious breads.

Cod roe Pressed cod roe is a cheap source of protein. It also contains small amounts of phosphorus, selenium, zinc, copper, iron, manganese and potassium.

Corned beef Don't write this one off just yet; corned beef is not as high in calories as you may think (although watch out for the fat content) and it's a good source of protein.

Crab Tinned crab is the most convenient way to eat it; although canning does dull the flavour somewhat, it's nothing that a dash of lemon juice and a shake of salt and pepper can't revive. Canning preserves crab's nutrients, and it is full of protein and omega-3 fatty acids.

Figs Not often found in tins, these are more commonly dried. They are an excellent source of fibre, and a good source of manganese and potassium.

Grapefruit A good source of vitamin C, fibre and potassium, grapefruit also contains carbohydrates, and the red and pink varieties contain lycopene (an antioxidant).

Green beans Botanically a member of the legumes family, green beans are a good source of fibre and vitamin B9, and a source of vitamins B2, C and E.

Haricot beans Also known as navy beans, haricot beans are an excellent source of dietary fibre and a very good source of both vitamin B9 and manganese. They are also a good source of many minerals including copper, phosphorus, magnesium and iron. In addition, they are a source of protein and vitamin B1.

Kidney beans These slightly ugly dark red-coloured nuggets are versatile powerhouses of goodness. Use them in anything from chillies to bean burgers, burritos to soups for a hefty whack of fibre, iron and the health-boosting vitamin B1. Due to their complex carbohydrate content they provide a slow-release of energy and are a source of protein.

Lemons (preserved) These are high in vitamin C, which isn't adversely affected by the process of preserving them. Unusually for a lemon you can eat the whole thing – skin and all – providing some extra fibre rather than just squeezing out the juice.

Lentils Due to their fibre content, lentils can help to lower cholesterol, which is part of the maintenance of cardiovascular health. The slow release of complex carbohydrates helps to stabilize blood glucose (sugar) levels. They are a good source of fibre, B vitamins including vitamin B9, protein, copper, iron and manganese.

Mackerel This is a good source of protein and omega-3 fatty acids, which play a role in the maintaining healthy hair, skin and nails.

Mandarins These are high in vitamin C, beta-carotene, dietary fibre and are a source of phosphorous.

Mushrooms Rich in B vitamins such as B1, B2, B3, B5 and B9. These help the body to release energy from digested food. They also aid in the formation of red blood cells.

Mussels These are a source of heart-healthy unsaturated fats. According to the author Joanna Blythman, regular consumption of mussels can help improve brain function and reduce inflammatory conditions such as arthritis.[2] Mussels are also a brilliant source of vitamins and packed with important minerals such as zinc, which helps build immunity. Mussels even contain levels of iron and vitamin B9 to rival red meats.

Olives Let me blow your mind: olives are classified (botanically) as a fruit! A tangy, bitter, fatty little fruit. They are also a good source of vitamin E and fibre as well as a source of monounsaturated fatty acids. According to the American Heart Association, 'monounsaturated fats can help reduce bad cholesterol levels in your blood which can lower your risk of heart disease and stroke.'

Peaches A good source of both fibre and vitamin C. A US study states that 'stone fruits such as peaches have been shown to ward off obesity-related diseases such as diabetes, metabolic syndrome and cardiovascular disease'.[3]

Pears A good source of vitamin C, as well as vitamin K, potassium and very small amounts of calcium, iron, magnesium, riboflavin, vitamin B6 and B9.

Peas Low in total and saturated fat, cholesterol and sodium, peas contain some protein; and vitamin A, C, K several B-vitamins including B2, B3, B6 and B9; magnesium, manganese, phosphorus, copper; and are a good source of dietary fibre.

Pineapple This contains some vitamins B1, B2, B5, B6 and B9, potassium and magnesium. Uniquely for a fruit, pineapple contains high quantities of manganese.

Pinto beans These are a good source of vitamin B1 and manganese; and contain some vitamin B9 and protein.

Potatoes Canned potatoes are a source of vitamins B6, C and fibre. They also contain some copper, potassium, manganese, phosphorous, vitamins B3 and B5.

Prunes These fruits are naturally high in fibre and contain small amounts of potassium in a standard serving of about 3 prunes (30g). Prunes are a good source of vitamin K and also contain some beta-carotene.

Pumpkin An 80g (3 tablespoons) serving of pumpkin provides an adult with a complete daily requirement of vitamin A. Pumpkins also contain some iron, fibre, vitamin C and are a good source of vitamin K.

Rhubarb Containing fibre and vitamin C, rhubarb is also a source of vitamin K and calcium.

Salmon Tinned salmon is high in protein and essential fatty acids, particularly omega-3 fatty acids. It is also a good source of selenium, calcium (if you eat the bones) and vitamins B2, B3, B6 and B12.

Sardines These little fish are a powerhouse of vitamins and nutrients; one small can contains the daily intake of vitamin B12 for an adult. Also rich in vitamins B2, B3 and D, selenium, phosphorous and calcium, omega-3 fatty acids and protein.

Spinach This leafy green vegetable is rich in vitamins B9 and C. Spinach contains vitamins A, B2 and E, protein, fibre, zinc, calcium and iron.

Sweetcorn Tinned sweetcorn contains fibre, vitamins B2, B3, B5 and C; magnesium; phosphorus and folic acid.

Tomatoes These are virtually fat- and cholesterol-free and are a source of vitamin C. They contain the antioxidants beta-carotene and lycopene that become more easily absorbed with cooking.[4]

Tuna An excellent source of selenium, vitamins B3 and B12 and protein, tuna is also a source of vitamin B2. It contains the minerals choline and iodine.

Yellow split peas Yellow split peas are a source of molybdenum. They are also a good source of dietary fibre, vitamin B9 and manganese, as well as a source of protein. They also contain smaller amounts of vitamin B5, phosphorus and potassium.

BUT WHAT DOES ALL THIS MEAN?[5]

Beta-carotene This is an antioxidant that is converted to vitamin A (also known as retinol) in the body, Vitamin A in its active form is very important for general overall health but especially healthy skin and mucus membranes, immunity and eye health. It is found in many brightly coloured red, yellow, orange and green fruits and vegetables.

Calcium Vital for the health of your bones and your teeth, calcium also plays a role in muscle function, enzyme reactions, hormone regulation, nerve function and the ability to form blood clots.

Copper We may know copper as a low-value coin, but it is also an essential nutrient for our bodies. (Please don't eat a fistful of pennies, though, as the jury is out on that one.) Working in conjunction with iron, copper enables the formation of red blood cells and helps to maintain healthy bones through enzyme reactions, the formation of new blood vessels, supporting nerve health and overall immunity.

Fibre Dietary fibre is important in maintaining normal digestive health and (sorry to bring it up, but we're all adults here!) regular bowel movements. Fibre helps you to feel fuller for longer, and a good amount of it in your daily diet can improve cholesterol and blood sugar levels and lower the risk of some diseases, such as diabetes, heart disease and bowel cancer.[6]

Iodine This is an essential nutrient for growth and development, fertility and metabolism through thyroid function.

Iron Forming part of the haemoglobin molecule in red blood cells that carries oxygen around the body, iron also plays a role in growth, cognitive function, healing of tissues and overall immune function.

Magnesium This supports the release of energy from digested foods, plays a vital role in the electrolyte composition of all body fluids, the production of hormones associated with blood glucose (sugar) regulation and is important in maintaining bone density.

Manganese This mineral helps with the formation of connective tissues, contributes to strong and healthy bones, assists with blood clotting and helps metabolize fat and carbohydrates. It also assists with the absorption of calcium and regulating blood sugar levels. Finally, it is vital for healthy brain and nerve function.

Omega-3 These fatty acids are predominantly found in oily fish, such as salmon, trout, sardines and mackerel. According to the American Heart Association, omega-3 fatty acids may reduce your risk of heart disease and stroke.[7]

Phosphorous Critical in maintaining the acid-base balance of your cells, phosphorus also supports the creation of bones and other mineral dense tissues, such as teeth. Phosphorus plays a role in energy storage and transfer.

Potassium This is a major, cell-based mineral (often referred to as an ion) that helps to maintain the correct fluid balance inside cells in conjunction with sodium. Potassium also works with sodium via the kidneys to maintain a healthy and consistent blood pressure. Lastly, it also plays a supporting role in maintaining acid-alkaline balance in the body.

Protein This is an essential macronutrient, just like carbohydrates and fats and vital component of all body tissues. Protein is both a building material that helps to form healthy bones, muscles, skin, connective tissue and other structures such as red blood cells but also forms the basis of other compounds such as enzymes that help to form reactions in our body and signally proteins (such as the blood sugar hormone insulin).

Selenium Regenerates the activity of vitamins C and E, contributes to your antioxidant activity and enhances your immune system. It also helps to prevent damage to your cells and tissues.

Sodium This is needed by the body to help balance fluid levels inside and outside of cells alongside potassium. Sodium also works indirectly to help digestion by supporting the production of enzymes in the pancreas. Table salt is also known as sodium chloride (sodium bound to chloride ions) and this is what is generally found in food (or sprinkled on it). According to the British Heart Foundation (BHF) having too much salt in our diet is linked to high blood pressure.[8] The BHF recommends consuming less than 6g of salt per day, so an easy way to do this is add less salt to your food and choose low-salt options where available.

Vitamin A (retinol) This vitamin is important for vision, the immune system and overall cellular health by protecting DNA, the genetic information in our cells from oxidative damage. Vitamin A also has a supporting role in helping the kidneys, heart and lungs to function properly and contributes to the maintenance of teeth, bones and other soft tissues.

Vitamin B1 (thiamine) Helps to produce energy for all the cells of our body, such as those found in the heart, muscles, brain and nervous system by supporting the body to release energy from our food.

Vitamin B2 (riboflavin) Vitamin B2 helps our bodies to break down and metabolise the energy from food and process certain neurotransmitters, such as dopamine, one of the 'feel good hormones'.

Vitamin B3 (niacin) Vitamin B3 supports over 200 enzyme reactions in the body including those in the release of energy from food. It is also important in the regeneration of the antioxidant glutathione (highly concentrated in the liver and brain) and vitamin C.

Vitamin B5 (pantothenic acid) More commonly called just pantothenic acid these days, vitamin B5 is a vital component part of an everyday diet helping to release energy from the food we eat but particularly fat metabolism.

Vitamin B6 (pyridoxine) Vitamin B6 is vital for brain development by helping to form certain fats called sphingolipids and also in the creation and operation of mitochondria (the tiny 'cells within cells' that help to create the energy currency of our body, adenosine triphosphate or ATP). Vitamin B6 helps the body to make serotonin as well as other hormones and neurotransmitters involved in stress and mood regulation.

Vitamin B9 (folate) Vital for human growth and development due to its role in rapidly growing tissues. Folate (also known as folic acid) is most commonly known as a supplemental vitamin for pregnant mothers to promote normal foetus growth and it does this by promoting normal nervous system development in the growing baby. Folate also supports the use of proteins and other vitamins (such as B12) for other body processes, such as the creation of red blood cells.

Vitamin B12 (cobalamin) This is needed for the health of all body cells but particularly it plays a crucial role in red blood cell and brain health. Vitamin B12 helps with the health of mitochondria and further improves the energy release from food.

Vitamin C (ascorbic acid) This plays a vital role in the formation of collagen (one of the proteins used in the connective tissue such as those in the skin). Vitamin C is also needed to produce certain hormones such as serotonin. Since vitamin C is an antioxidant, it helps to protect cells from damage, such as those caused by pollution.

Vitamin D (cholecalciferol and ergocalciferol) According to the NHS website, 'vitamin D helps regulate the amount of calcium and phosphate in the body. These nutrients are needed to keep bones, teeth and muscles healthy.'[9] From March through to September, most people can obtain all the vitamin D they need through natural sunlight, but for the rest of the year we need to help our supply by introducing vitamin D sources, such as oily fish and fortified foods, into our diet.

Vitamin E (tocopherol) Helps to maintain the integrity or strength of cells through it's natural antioxidant ability. In this way vitamin E is crucial in maintaining delicate tissues such as healthy skin, eyes and the sexual organs. As an antioxidant, vitamin E also plays a supporting role in the body's defence system against damaging 'oxidants' such as pollution.

Vitamin K (phylloquinone and menaquinone) This is essential in blood clotting process by working with other 'clotting factors' in the blood stream which helps to stop bleeding and for the wound to heal properly. Vitamin K also plays a role in structural protein formation, so it helps to strengthen bones, cartilage and teeth.

Zinc This mineral has many body processes, such as the production of new cells, repairing tissues, immunity through various mechanisms, supporting normal blood sugar regulation, protein synthesis and very importantly, taste! Zinc helps to manage taste sensitivity and a deficiency can lead to taste disturbances.

BREAKFAST & BRUNCH

SPINACH BAKED EGGS

SERVES 2

1 x 400g tin of chopped tomatoes

1 tbsp oil

1 x 400g tin of spinach

1 tbsp garlic paste or 2 fat cloves of garlic, crushed (optional)

1 tsp curry powder, mild, medium, or as hot as you dare

2–4 eggs

salt and pepper

This is a simpler take on a shakshuka, which is a popular Mediterranean and Middle Eastern dish thought to have originated in Tunisia. A typical shakshuka contains peppers, so if you have any fresh, frozen or jarred peppers kicking about, feel free to add those too. Onion also goes well in this, or you can add any scraps of vegetables you may have.

First pour the tomatoes and oil into a large, shallow pan. Open the spinach, drain if required, and spoon it in, stirring well to combine. Add the garlic, if using, and curry powder. Pop the pan over a medium heat and cook for 15 minutes.

Using a spoon, make a hole for each egg in the spinach-tomato mixture. Crack in the eggs and cover the pan to cook the top – I often cover mine with a second pan or a sturdy plate if I don't have a lid for it.

Poach the eggs in the sauce for around 6 minutes, until the whites are firm and the yolks still slightly runny, then season with a little salt and pepper and serve.

CHEEKY CORN FRITTERS

V

SERVES 2–4, DEPENDING ON APPETITE

1 small onion, finely chopped or 100g frozen sliced onion

75g self-raising flour

⅛ tsp cayenne pepper or ¼ tsp chilli powder

salt and pepper

300g drained, tinned sweetcorn

2 eggs

2 tbsp milk or water

2 tbsp cooking oil

A good corn fritter recipe is an excellent thing to have up your sleeve, for breakfast, brunch, or making a meal out of a tin of corn. This is as good a recipe as any, and once you know how to do it, you'll never be short of a speedy, filling brunch recipe.

Toss the onion into a large mixing bowl. Add the flour, cayenne pepper or chilli powder, salt and pepper, and stir well to coat it all. Add the sweetcorn to the bowl and stir again. Crack in the eggs and add the milk or water, then mix well to form a rough batter.

Heat the oil in a large frying pan on a medium heat. Drop in the batter, 2–3 tablespoons at a time. Cook for 3–4 minutes on each side, and serve.

HOMEMADE BAKED BEANS
VE

SERVES 2

1 x 400g tin of baked beans

100g frozen sliced onion, or 1 small onion, finely sliced

1 x 400g tin of chopped tomatoes

1 tbsp oil

a pinch of salt

1 tsp vinegar

1 tsp sugar

Some might argue the logic behind rinsing the sauce from a tin of baked beans, only to replace it with your own. It seems a lot of effort to go to just for something slightly superior, but slightly superior it is. I love these – on their own on toast, spooned into a pitta bread, or as part of a big breakfast – and they're three of your five-a-day, too.

First tip your beans into a sieve or colander and run them under a cold tap to get rid of all the sticky orange sauce. Tip them into a medium saucepan.

Add the onion to the pan, then add the remaining ingredients and turn the heat to medium for 5 minutes until the sauce starts to gently bubble. Stir gently with a wooden spoon to stop everything sticking and burning on the bottom. Cook for a further 15 minutes until the sauce is thick and glossy, then serve.

These beans can be cooled and frozen for up to 6 months, or kept in the fridge, covered, for up to 3 days.

CARROT CAKE OVERNIGHT OATS

V

SERVES 2

200g drained, tinned carrots

250ml milk

70g porridge oats

70g dried sultanas or mixed peel

½ tsp ground cinnamon

2 tbsp sugar (optional but delicious)

Overnight oats became something of a phenomenon a couple of years ago; the act of soaking porridge oats overnight in milk or yoghurt with a topping of choice. I like my breakfasts to resemble desserts as often as possible, so I started to play with classic cake combinations to make this healthy start a little more appetizing. This version, although it tastes decadent, contains two of your five-a-day, and is very simple to throw together. Tinned carrots work better than fresh here, as their softness makes them easier to blend.

Tip the carrots into a blender with the milk. Blend until smooth; the milk will turn a glorious soft peach colour. This is carrot milk; bizarre, but for our purposes in this recipe, absolutely perfect.

Stir in the porridge oats and sultanas or mixed peel, cinnamon and sugar, if using. Mix well. Pour into a large jar with a lid or other suitable container that will hold double its volume – the oats will absorb the liquid and swell. Cover and place in the fridge to chill for at least 8 hours, or overnight.

Serve chilled with a splash of extra milk, or cream if you're feeling particularly decadent and happen to have some to hand.

RHUBARB & CUSTARD PANCAKES
V

SERVES 4

350g self-raising flour

½ tsp salt

1 tsp bicarbonate of soda or 2 tbsp baking powder

300g tinned custard

300ml milk (UHT is fine)

2 eggs

½ x 600g tin of rhubarb – use the rest on top!

butter or oil, for cooking

My little family loves pancakes and I try to come up with new ones every weekend for them to try, eaten in bed with the weekend newspapers and a comic for Small Boy. These were a particular hit; although the first time I made them I blended the rhubarb in a small bullet blender to make it less detectable for my increasingly fussy son.

First combine the flour, salt and bicarbonate of soda or baking powder in a large mixing bowl, and stir well to evenly distribute.

In a separate bowl, pour in the custard and thin with a little of the milk. Add the rest of the milk gradually, stirring, until it is all incorporated in a loose, liquidy mixture. If you have a small blender, you can whizz them together in that, but I do it by hand to save on washing up. You have to do it slowly, though, or else you run the risk of ending up with a milk soup and lumps of custard floating in it, so patience is a virtue here!

Make a well – a sort of hole – in the centre of the dry ingredients. Tip in the custardy milk, crack in the eggs and mix well to form a thick batter.

Drain the rhubarb, keeping the syrup to drizzle on the pancakes later. Tip the rhubarb into the pancake mix and stir briskly. Pop the whole lot in the fridge to chill out for half an hour or so – the best pancakes are made when cold, cold batter hits a hot, hot pan, because … science.

When the batter is nice and chilled, preheat your oven to 160°C (fan 140°C/320°F/gas 3) and place a clean baking tray on the middle shelf. This is so that you can keep your pancakes warm as you cook them in batches, and it also gives them a little rise, for extra fluffy thickness.

Warm the largest frying pan that you can find. Dollop in a little butter or oil, and crank that heat up until it's hot but not smoking. Turn the heat OFF immediately if it starts to smoke, remove the pan, allow it to cool, rinse it with cold water and start again. Always opt for five seconds' inconvenience over a potential house fire, and pay close attention to your pan!

When the pan is hot, dollop a hefty spoon of batter onto it, and another, and another, leaving a gap between each pancake to allow you to turn them over. Cook for a few minutes until light golden and starting to set before turning them over with a spatula, and cook for a few minutes more. Transfer to your warm baking tray while you cook the rest. When all the batter is used up, serve with the reserved syrup, and enjoy.

TIPS
The rhubarb can be replaced with the same quantity of any very soft tinned fruit. To make the pancakes vegan, simply replace the egg with applesauce and use plant-based milk and soya custard.

GET UP & GO SMOOTHIE

V

SERVES 1

8 tinned prunes

40g porridge oats

250ml milk

The oats in this quick and effective breakfast form the 'get up' portion, being a good source of slow-release energy, and the prunes – well – they should speak for themselves! This makes for a swift but stimulating start to the day, in every imaginable sense. Not one for the long-distance commuter, perhaps...

First remove the stones from the prunes, then pop the fruits into your blender. Add the oats and milk, and blend until smooth – or as smooth as it gets. Down it in one; you're ready for anything now!

TIP

Blenders are pretty handy to have in the kitchen. If you don't have one, you can sometimes pick them up from charity shops for a song and they'll usually have PAT tested them so they won't go bang.

TIN CAN COOK

CANNED OJ
VE

SERVES 1

1 tin of mandarins
(any size), drained

This is so simple and so sweet, and an excellent hit of
vitamin C. Tinned mandarins give this juice a luscious
honey note with a tangy finish – and all hiding in a
humble tin.

Toss the mandarins into a small blender. Half-fill the tin with
water and add it to the mandarins, then blend until smooth.
If you like your juice with 'no bits', simply pour it through a sieve
to catch them.

Chill it in the fridge or freezer, and stir before serving in case
it separates. I drink mine at room temperature because I'm
impatient, but it is nicer chilled or served over a little ice.

TIP
*This method works with most tinned fruits, so experiment
and enjoy!*

MANGO & COCONUT PORRIDGE

VE

SERVES 4

250g drained, tinned mango slices

1 x 400g tin of coconut milk

120g porridge oats

a pinch of sugar, to serve (optional)

As a food writer, I happen to have a well-stocked spice collection, so I'll admit to adding a pinch of ground cardamom or cinnamon to this recipe if the mood takes me. It isn't mandatory, however; the sweet and silky mango and coconut flavours are quite big enough on their own. This porridge sings of summer while being cosy and comforting for winter; and the juice from the mango tin is a treat all of its own – simply dilute and drink it!

Pop the mango slices into a medium saucepan. You are going to stew your mango to make a compote – this is best described as looking like a cross between a crumble base and a soft-set jam. Cook the fruit on a low–medium heat for 10 minutes, mashing it with a fork as it softens.

Tip in the coconut milk and the oats and stir well. Bring carefully to an almost-boil, then lower the heat to a simmer. Fill the coconut milk tin with water and add a little at a time to the saucepan, stirring, as the oats start to absorb it and swell.

Continue to add the water as you cook the porridge for around 10 more minutes, stirring continually to stop it sticking and burning, until it is at your desired consistency. Serve warm with a pinch of sugar, if you like.

TIP

If you're not vegan, you could use milk in the porridge instead of water – it makes a very rich porridge.

PINA COLADA BREAD
VE

MAKES 1 ENORMOUS LOAF

2 tsp dried active yeast

1 x approx 400g tin of pineapple chunks, drained (retain the juice for another time)

500ml coconut milk (or 1 x 400g tin of coconut milk plus 100ml water)

750g self-raising flour, plus extra for dusting

butter or oil, for greasing

I first made this on a dismal October morning after a long, uncharacteristically hot summer that had beamed in from mid-May until that particular drizzly day. My normally bright home was grey and miserable, and I yearned for the weather of the weeks and months before. Looking to inject some sunshine into my mood, I surveyed my tin collection and plucked out pineapples and coconut milk, and the Pina Colada bread was born. This recipe makes a rather large loaf; leftovers make for a phenomenal bread and butter pudding.

First activate your yeast; give it a little warm bath to encourage it into life. Don't make it too hot, though; the optimum temperature is somewhere around 40°C, or just comfortably warm. Too hot and you'll kill off the yeast, which means your bread will sulk and refuse to rise. So pop it into a small cup with 50ml warm water, and leave it for a few minutes, to start to bubble and grow.

In the meantime, blitz the pineapple chunks and coconut milk in a blender. This step is not strictly essential; if you don't have a blender you can use the pineapple chunks whole, which makes for a different result but still a deliciously pleasant one. However you use it, tip the coconut milk and pineapple into a large mixing bowl. Add half the flour, and the warm yeast mixture, and mix swiftly, but firmly, to form a batter.

→

Gradually incorporate the remaining flour into the mixture, a large heaped spoonful at a time, until a dough is formed. I have made many loaves of bread over the years and have found that a non-serrated butter knife is the best implement to bring a dough together, as it doesn't stick awkwardly to any edges. If you don't have one, the well-oiled handle of a clean wooden spoon works just as well. It will feel a little odd at first, but it works!

When you have a soft, squashy dough, heavily flour your worktop and tip the dough carefully onto it. Knead it for around 5 minutes, pushing it away from you with the palm of your hand, then folding it in half, giving it a quarter turn, and repeating, getting faster as you gain a little confidence with it. You should feel a change in the texture of the dough as you knead it; it will become springy and slightly buoyant to touch – this is when you need to stop and leave it alone! Scoop it back into the mixing bowl and cover with cling film or a loosely plonked plastic bag with the handles tucked beneath the bowl. (You need to make sure no air can escape and dry out the dough.)

Leave it to rise for 2 hours in a warm place, or 3 in a not-so-warm one. If your kitchen is generally cold, wrap the base of the bowl in a thick towel or fluffy dressing gown to snuggle it and get it going.

When risen, the dough should be doubled in size. Shape it into a round or a log, pop it on a greased baking tray or into a large, greased cake tin (I like to use a 1-litre bundt tin or 900g loaf tin). Leave it for another hour to prove – that's a second rise.

Preheat your oven to 170°C (fan 150°C/320°F/gas 3) about 10 minutes before the proving hour is up, and make sure there is a shelf positioned just below the middle of the oven.

Pop the bread in for 1 hour, until risen and golden. Remove from the tray or tip out of the tin and allow to cool on a wire rack. Enjoy warm, or cool. Store leftovers in an airtight bag or container for up to 3 days, or in the freezer, in slices, for up to 6 months.

TIP

For real Pina Colada authenticity, spread the bread with butter spiked with a little cinnamon and rum.

SOUPS

CREAMY TOMATO SOUP
VE

SERVES 2 HEARTILY

200g drained and rinsed tinned carrots

1 x 400g tin of tomatoes

½ x 400g tin coconut milk

1 vegetable stock cube

black pepper (optional)

This vegan version of a cream of tomato soup uses three tins and a stock cube and nothing else. For best results you will need a blender, but if you don't have one, you can mash the carrots with a fork and have a slightly less smooth, but still delicious, soup.

Toss the carrots into a blender with the tinned tomatoes. Blend together to make a smooth liquid, then pour this into a saucepan. Add the coconut milk and crumble in the stock cube. Bring to a low heat – no higher just yet as the soup will spoil if boiled – and cook for 15 minutes to meld the flavours together and slightly reduce the liquid.

When ready to serve, blast the soup quickly on a high heat for just a minute, and serve piping hot. I like to add a little black pepper to mine, but it is perfectly fine just as it is.

EASY GAZPACHO
VE

SERVES 2

½ cucumber, diced (peeled if you like, but it isn't necessary)

½ onion, finely sliced, or 70g frozen sliced onion

1 tbsp garlic paste or 2 fat cloves of garlic, crushed

2 x 400g tins of chopped tomatoes

4 tbsp oil

1 tsp sugar

1 tbsp vinegar

salt and pepper

I've simplified gazpacho here, in keeping with the spirit of the book; the original usually contains a red or orange pepper and some freshly chopped herbs. You can add both, or neither, as you like.

Place about a quarter of the cucumber, onion and garlic in a bowl and cover with cling film. Put the rest of the cucumber, onion and garlic, with the tomatoes, in a blender.

Add the oil, sugar, vinegar and seasoning. Blend everything at top speed until the soup is absolutely smooth.

Taste to check the seasoning, adjust if necessary with more salt and pepper, and pour into a large bowl. Stir in a little cold water to thin it slightly – 150–275ml as required. Pop the soup into the fridge and chill thoroughly.

When you're ready to serve, ladle the soup into the bowls and scatter over the reserved vegetables.

CARROT AND GINGER SOUP
VE

SERVES 2

100g frozen sliced onion or 1 small onion, finely sliced

1 tbsp garlic paste or 2 fat cloves of garlic, crushed

a small piece of fresh root ginger, grated, or 1 tbsp of the lazy stuff

1 tbsp oil

300g drained, tinned carrots

1 vegetable stock cube

salt and pepper

1 tsp lemon juice

This simple soup is one I make often when I'm a little peckish, need lunch in a hurry, or want some simple goodness. You can use fresh carrots in place of tinned ones if you have them, but the benefit of tinned means that they are already cooked and sliced, making this the work of a moment.

First pop the onion in a large saucepan. Add the garlic, ginger and the oil and cook on a very low heat for 5 minutes to start to soften.

Tip the carrots into the pan. Add 400ml water, crumble in the stock cube and bring to the boil. Cook for 15 minutes until everything is softened.

Tip the contents of the pan into a blender and pulse until smooth. Return the soup to the pan and warm through. Season with a little salt and pepper and a dash of lemon juice, stir through, and serve.

CREAMY 'CHICKEN' SOUP

SERVES 2, IF A 220G TIN IS USED

tin of pease pudding

hot chicken stock

milk

garlic paste

pepper

(There are no measurements given for this recipe, because it all depends on the size of your tin)

I first discovered this while fiddling with a tin of pease pudding: yellow split peas soaked and cooked to a mush and pressed into a can in a homogenous layer of firm slop, with a hint of turmeric. I plopped it into a pan, stared at it, and wondered what the ever-loving flip I could do to make it edible, let alone enjoyable. A can of milk and another of chicken stock later, along with a hefty dose of garlic and pepper, and I had the most convincingly creamy chicken soup – with barely a snifter of chicken in it. Curious and curiouser.

First grab a medium saucepan and boil the kettle to make your stock.

Open the tin of pease pudding and prise it into the pan. Fill the tin two-thirds full with hot stock, and pour it into the pan. Refill the tin two-thirds full with milk, and stand to one side for a moment. The milk, not you. Add garlic to taste – for a small tin I would recommend 1 level tablespoon of paste, for anything larger, as much as you dare.

Turn the heat to medium, and break up the pease pudding with a fork or wooden spoon. Beat thoroughly; the pease pudding will start to dissolve into the stock. It does take a little effort but it will get there eventually, with continuous stirring.

When the soup is smooth, gradually add the milk – being careful not to let it boil over as the milk will burn and leave a sour taste, so turn the heat down a little. When the milk is all incorporated, remove from the heat, season with a little pepper, and serve.

ROASTED TOMATO, WHITE BEAN & MANDARIN SOUP

VE

SERVES 2

2 x 400g tins of chopped tomatoes

1 x 300g tin of mandarins

100g frozen sliced onion or 1 small onion, finely sliced

1 x 400g tin of cannellini or haricot beans, drained and rinsed

1 tbsp garlic paste or 4 cloves of garlic

salt and pepper

1 vegetable stock cube dissolved in 200ml boiling water

dried thyme or rosemary, to serve

This soup is an unusual one, but it works well. It's filling, sweet, hearty and a glorious colour! You can cook it in a pan instead of roasting it if using the oven for an hour is a concern; it won't have the same underlying caramelly depth of flavour, but it will still be a delicious warming bowl of soup.

Preheat the oven to 180°C (fan 160°C/350°F/gas 4).

Grab the largest roasting tin or casserole dish that you have that will fit in the oven, and tip in the tins of tomatoes. Drain the mandarins, keeping the juice to one side to add later, and tip those in too. Tip in the onion, beans and garlic and season with a little salt and pepper. (It will look like a lovely mix of ingredients as per the illustration opposite.)

Stir well to evenly distribute the ingredients, pop the roasting tin into the oven and cook for 25 minutes, stirring halfway through.

When cooked, carefully transfer the contents to a blender and pulse until smooth. Pour into a large saucepan; you may need to do this in batches!

When the fruit and veg is all blended, warm the soup through and thin it with a little veg stock and the reserved mandarin juice, a splash at a time. Season with extra pepper and a little thyme or rosemary, to serve.

WHITE BEAN, SPINACH & GARLIC SOUP

VE

SERVES 2

1 x 400g tin of cannellini or haricot beans (butter beans at a push)

150g frozen or tinned spinach

1 vegetable stock cube

2 tbsp garlic paste or 4 fat cloves of garlic, roughly chopped

1 onion, finely sliced, or 100g frozen sliced onion

1 tbsp lemon juice

black pepper

I'll admit, this looks utterly horrendous. An effulgent quagmire (a fancy way of saying 'swampy swamp') of marshy green slop, somewhere on the imaginary colour chart between Tarragon's Breath and Poisoned Paradise.

A looker it certainly isn't, but as my mother always told me, it's what's inside that counts. And what's inside this is a flavour bang of bright greens, musky garlic, creamy soft beans, a zing of lemon and pepper and a whole host of vitamins and goodness to boot. I prefer it made with frozen spinach, as tinned tastes, well, a little grassy to my sensitive tastebuds, but it works if there's nothing else in.

First drain your beans, retaining the liquor for other recipes (see Tip opposite). Rinse the beans, and pop them in a medium or large saucepan. Add the spinach, 350ml water and the crumbled stock cube, and bring to the boil – big rolling bubbles. Reduce to a simmer.

Add the garlic and onion to the pan and simmer for 20 minutes, stirring occasionally, until the beans are nice and soft and creamy.

Remove from the heat and tip into a blender. Blend until smooth – you may need a little splash more water to get it to your desired consistency.

When the soup is smooth, return it to the saucepan. Heat for a few minutes to warm it back through. Finish with a little lemon juice and black pepper to bring it to life, and enjoy.

TIP

You can retain the bean liquor to use as an egg replacement in glazing pastry, biscuits or even meringue – it's called aquafaba, and it's a revelation. It keeps for a week or so in the fridge in a tightly sealed jar.

TIN-ESTRONE
VE

SERVES 2

1 onion, diced, or 100g frozen sliced onion

1 tbsp garlic paste or 2 fat cloves of garlic, crushed

200g drained, tinned carrots

1 tbsp oil

1 x 400g tin of chopped tomatoes

1 vegetable stock cube dissolved in 600ml boiling water

½ tsp mixed dried herbs

1 x 400g tin of baked beans

1 x 400g tin of spaghetti hoops in tomato sauce

Minestrone. From tins. Not much more to say other than I apologise for my terrible taste in jokes, which I hope redeems itself in my excellent taste in soup.

Toss the onion and garlic into a heavy-bottomed saucepan with the carrots and pour over the oil. Stir and cook over a medium heat for around 5 minutes to start to soften the veg.

When the veg have started to soften, pour over the chopped tomatoes and the stock. Crank the heat right up, toss in the mixed dried herbs and bring it all to the boil. When it's bubbling away, stir it well, and reduce to medium heat and simmer for a few minutes.

Meanwhile, gently rinse the tomato sauce off the baked beans and spaghetti hoops, taking care as the spaghetti can be a bit fragile, then tip into the pan and stir through. Cook for a further 10 minutes until the beans have softened and it's looking good! It's definitely not authentic, but it'll do.

LENTIL & CHESTNUT SOUP

SERVES 4–6

2 tbsp oil

100g frozen sliced onion or 1 small onion, finely sliced

200g drained, tinned carrots, diced

1 x 400g tin of brown or green lentils, drained and rinsed

2 vegetable stock cubes dissolved in 1.5 litres boiling water

1 x 180g pack of cooked chestnuts, whole or chopped

a handful of chopped fresh parsley (optional)

a dash of milk, to serve

This recipe is adapted from *How To Eat* by Nigella Lawson, who in turn adapted it from 'an aromatic, velvety, manilla-coloured soup at Le Caprice' in the late 1980s. The bootstrap adjustments and pricing are my own. The original recipe includes half a leek, which I have omitted out of laziness; I didn't have one in and didn't want to take a trip to the shop especially, but if you want to stick more closely to the original, slice it and add it at the same time as the onion.

Heat the oil in a large saucepan and add the chopped vegetables. Cook over a low heat to allow them to soften for around 10 minutes.

Add the lentils to the pan, pour over the stock, and bring to the boil. Reduce to a simmer and continue to cook until the lentils are soft and swollen – usually around 30 minutes.

Add the chestnuts and simmer for 20 more minutes. Transfer to a blender – in batches if need be – and liquidize until smooth.

Tip back into the pan and stir through the parsley, if using. If you're feeling particularly fancy, stir through a tablespoon or two of milk to finish.

TIP

If chestnuts are a step too far outside of your comfort zone, replace these with a couple of tablespoonfuls of peanut butter instead; this variation benefits from the addition of a hefty whack of dried chilli flakes and lemon juice just before serving, turning it into an entirely different meal, but a delicious one.

SUNSHINE SOUP
VE

SERVES 2

1 x 400g tin of
cannellini beans

200g tinned or
frozen sweetcorn

1 vegetable stock
cube

100g frozen sliced
onion or 1 small
onion, finely sliced

1 tbsp garlic paste, or
2 fat cloves of garlic,
crushed

1 tbsp ground
turmeric

1 tsp paprika

1 tbsp grated fresh
root ginger, or 1 tsp
ground ginger

black pepper

This is a veritable hug in a mug, an incandescent combustion of luminosity; the holy triumvirate of garlic, turmeric and ginger to banish any sniffles and blues. Made simply from a tin of beans, a tin of sweetcorn and some frippery around the edges, as with so many simple recipes, this is so much more than the sum of its humble parts. If you find yourself lacking one or two of the flavour components – say there's no turmeric kicking around or the paprika pot is bare – you can just leave them out. A little curry powder works in place of all of the odds and sods, in a pinch.

First drain the cannellini beans. (You can retain the liquor from the tin, see Tip on page 49.) Rinse the beans and pop them in a medium saucepan. Add the sweetcorn, cover with 400ml water and crumble in the stock cube. Bring to the boil, then reduce to a simmer.

Add the onion to the pan with the garlic, turmeric, paprika and ginger, and simmer all together for 20 minutes to really soften the beans.

Remove from the heat and transfer to a blender, including all the liquor from the cooking pot. Pulse until smooth – this may take a few goes as sweetcorn skins are hardy little blighters – and pour back into the pan. Warm through and serve with a shake of black pepper.

SPICED LENTIL & KIDNEY BEAN SOUP

V

SERVES 4

1 x 400g tin of brown or green lentils, drained and rinsed

1 x 400g tin of kidney beans in water, drained and rinsed

100g frozen sliced onion or 1 small onion, finely sliced

1–2 tbsp garlic paste, or 4 fat cloves of garlic, crushed

a few thin slices of fresh root ginger, or 1 tbsp lazy ginger

1 small red chilli, finely sliced, or a pinch of dried chilli flakes

1 tsp ground turmeric

2 tsp ground cumin

a pinch of salt

2 tbsp oil

400ml vegetable stock

1 x 400g tin of chopped tomatoes

dash of milk (optional)

Based on the flavours of a Dal Makhani, this soup is warming and filling; ideal for autumnal lunches all the way through to the first buds of spring. It freezes beautifully and develops in flavour as it sits, so do make a large batch of it, and enjoy!

Tip the lentils and beans into a large pan and add the onion and garlic. Add the ginger, then the chilli, turmeric, cumin and salt.

Add the oil, then cook over a medium heat for 5–6 minutes to start to soften the garlic and onions. Stir well to incorporate the spices.

Add the stock and tomatoes. Bring to the boil, then reduce to a simmer and cook for 20 minutes to soften the lentils, beans and veg.

Once cooked, transfer to a blender and pulse until smooth. Tip back into the pan. Thin with a little water or, if you prefer a creamy soup, a dash of milk.

Serve hot, or allow to cool and then freeze for up to 6 months. Will keep for up to 3 days in the fridge, stored in a clean jar, sealed bag or other suitably airtight container.

SPICY RICE & TWO BEAN SOUP
VE

**SERVES 4
GENEROUSLY**

100g fresh or frozen diced peppers

1 x 400g tin of tomatoes

1 x 400g tin of white beans or baked beans, drained and rinsed

a little oil

salt

300ml vegetable stock

100g plain rice

1 x 400g tin of kidney beans, drained and rinsed

1 tsp paprika

¼ tsp ground black pepper

1 tbsp lemon juice or vinegar

This soup was a soup to shake me out of a funk longer than any I have recently known. I had a serious accident one Saturday night and hit my head backwards on a concrete floor at some speed. I ended up with whiplash and concussion, both of which limited my ability to sleep and work – and in the case of the latter, have so much as a thought in my head.

For the first few days I rather enjoyed the peace and quiet of absolute mental vacancy as my brain shut itself down to heal, but I also temporarily lost my ability to create – the thundering hum of a thousand ideas that usually fly around at any given time, as I clutch at them wildly, trying to capture one to expand on. And they vanished, to be replaced with absolutely nothing at all.

I lived off crisps and apathy for a week – and being miserable – until on the seventh day I felt like wandering into the kitchen. I threw this together from what I had to hand, and it was exactly what I needed. Easy, thick, hearty, filling and packed with spice and flavour. And wholesome and hearty enough to not be reaching for snacks – or even thinking about dinner – five hours later.

This is going to be my new self-care soup, for down days, and I highly recommend it.

Preheat the oven to 180°C (fan 160°C/350°F/gas 4).

To make the base: toss the peppers into a roasting tin, then add the tomatoes and white or baked beans and place in the oven for 20 minutes, with a little shake of oil and a pinch of salt to bring them to life.

When cooked, tip into a blender with the vegetable stock and blitz until roughly smooth. It doesn't have to be perfectly smooth; this is a chunky and hearty soup, so it doesn't have to be perfect.

Tip the soup into a pan and bring it to the boil, then reduce to a simmer (while you quickly wash up the blender jug – see Tip below). Add the rice and give everything a good stir.

Tip in the kidney beans and add the paprika, pepper and lemon juice or vinegar. Simmer for 20 minutes, stirring intermittently to stop the rice sticking to the base of the pan. Serve when the rice is soft and swollen.

TIPS

In a real funk, you can replace the uncooked rice with a bag of microwave rice, which slightly increases the cost but reduces the effort. If you do this, you will need to reduce the amount of stock by around half, as it won't be absorbed by the rice.

Blender jugs are far easier to clean when freshly used than trying to scrape caked-on crap off the sides of it later on. I put a splosh of water and a squirt of washing-up liquid in mine, return it to the base and re-blend it – it is practically self-cleaning!

BEANS

SWEET–SOUR CANNELLINIS
VE

MAKES 1 JAR

1 x 400g tin of cannellini beans, drained and rinsed

½ small onion, finely sliced – fresh is best here but 50g frozen sliced onion will suffice

100g frozen peppers or 1 small pepper of any colour, finely chopped

80ml vinegar – red, white or cider

1 tbsp white sugar

100ml oil – olive is admittedly best but vegetable or sunflower will suffice

I first came across the idea of sweet-sour pickled beans in Sarah Raven's *Garden Cookbook*, a treasure trove of favourite recipes organised by the seasons and by individual ingredient type. A veritable encyclopedia of inspiration and information, I often casually flick through to find new ways of using familiar products, and this recipe was one of them. Friends rave about these beans; they request them, they gratefully receive jars of them as gifts. The recipe may seem simple but the end result is nothing short of spectacular. And the recipe is so adaptable, I have made these with many different beans; Sarah prefers borlotti, while I opt for cannellini, for their creamy richness and satisfying heft. I'm yet to brave the butter bean, however.

Pop the beans into a pan of cold water. Bring to the boil, then reduce the heat to a simmer. Simmer for 15 minutes to really soften the beans, then drain them thoroughly and set aside.

Meanwhile, thoroughly clean and sterilize a large jar (at least 800ml in size) and its lid. You can sterilize with Milton fluid, used for cleaning baby bottles and useful to keep in the kitchen, or by washing with hot soapy water and baking in the oven for 10 minutes at 120°C (fan 100°C/250°F/gas ½), jar and lid together.

Place the beans in the sterilized jar.

Add the chopped onion and pepper to the pan, along with the vinegar, sugar and oil. Bring the pan to the boil very, very carefully, do not take your eyes off it for a moment as you are dealing with hot oil and it poses a fire risk if unattended.

As soon as bubbles start to form, remove the pan from the heat immediately.

Allow the mixture to cool for a minute, stirring well, then pour into the sterilized jar over the beans, as full as you can get it. Pop the lid on and turn the jar upside down to cool (Sarah suggests this), then allow to cool completely before placing in the fridge.

Try to resist sampling them for at least 7 days, as the flavour will develop in this time. If the jar is clean and sterile, these can keep for a few months unopened. Once opened, use within a week.

TIP
Eat these warmed on toast, on a salad, as a side dish, chilled and straight from the fridge, as a midnight snack, tapas – there is no occasion on which these will not beautifully, deliciously suit.

BOSTON-STYLE BEANS

SERVES 2

1 x 400g tin of baked beans

1 tbsp garlic paste or 2 fat cloves of garlic, crushed

100g frozen sliced onion or 1 small onion, finely sliced

1 x 400g tin of chopped tomatoes

½ tsp paprika

1 tsp vinegar, plus a splash to serve

170g (approx) tinned pork or ham

These aren't exactly authentic Boston beans, but they are porky and smoky, so I've taken the liberty of giving them this title. When I started writing this book, we were on the cusp of a looming food crisis, where senior politicians predicted food shortages as Britain was due to leave the European Union, and I started to reimagine my favourite classic recipes as though I only had a pantry of tinned food at my disposal. This was one of them. (There is a nine-month discrepancy between writing a cookbook and it being published, so lord knows what will have happened by the time you come to read this, but here's a recipe for emergency beans regardless of the current political landscape!)

I don't bother rinsing the sauce from the baked beans for this recipe; the saccharine-sweet base note is part of its appeal. So, tip the beans and sauce straight into a saucepan, and bring to a medium heat. Add the garlic, onion, tomatoes, paprika and vinegar and stir well.

Separately, grate the ham or pork on the 'large hole' side of a box grater. Pop it into the pan with the beans and stir it in. Cook for a further 10 minutes; the ham will start to dissolve slightly, which is fine. Add a splash of water if required to stop the sauce drying out too much. Cook for a further 10 minutes, then serve, with a splash of vinegar to finish.

These beans can be cooled and frozen in a freezerproof container for up to 6 months, or kept in the fridge, covered, for up to 3 days.

CHICKPEAS WITH BREAD & SPINACH
VE

SERVES 2

1 x 400g tin of chickpeas, drained and rinsed

4 tbsp oil or 60g butter

2 tbsp garlic paste, or 4 fat cloves of garlic, crushed

1 tbsp paprika

1 tbsp ground cumin or garam masala

100g bread, torn or chopped into 2.5cm chunks

1 x 400g tin of spinach

400ml vegetable stock

salt and pepper

This is my favourite recipe for using up old greens and bread. Any bean will do; I've used chickpeas here but kidney beans make for an earthy, serious bite, and cannellinis lend a creamy luxury as they start to fall apart in the pan. Tinned spinach looks utterly petrifying when you first peel back the lid, but it's perfect for this. If the idea really rankles, use 400g frozen or a few handfuls of fresh, but you get more for your money with a tin.

Toss the chickpeas into a large pan. Add the oil or butter, garlic and spices, and cook for 3–4 minutes on a medium heat, stirring to incorporate the spices.

Toss the bread pieces into the pan. Drain the spinach if required (I have found that most tinned spinach is very tightly packed and needs no draining, but I haven't tested every single brand!) and add that too. Pour over the stock and season generously with salt and pepper.

Bring to the boil, then reduce to a simmer and cook for 20–30 minutes until the bread is swollen and the liquid has been absorbed. Enjoy warm or chilled – it makes a fantastic filling for wraps or pitta breads, a decent lunch or a side dish for curriess. You can blitz leftovers into a hearty, homely soup.

BREAD, BEAN & HERB STEW
VE

SERVES 2-4

1 x 400g tin of white beans, drained and rinsed

300g drained and rinsed tinned carrots

1 x 400g tin of chopped tomatoes

1 tbsp garlic paste or 2 cloves of garlic, crushed

300ml vegetable stock

½ tsp mixed dried herbs

2 slices of bread, torn or cut into small chunks

salt and pepper

1 tsp lemon juice

The idea of putting bread in stew is one that dates back hundreds of years, to a medieval broth drink known as 'caudle'. It is both a use-up for stale bread, or crusts cut off for fussy children, and adds texture and thickness to a liquid broth. This soup is hearty, wholesome and delicious and made in a grey January fog for a group of hungry friends and devoured with gusto.

The ingredients are all fairly interchangeable; the beans can be any kind you fancy, even plain old baked beans will do. I make mine with kidney beans sometimes, but baked beans are my favourite smutty staple in soups and stews. You can extend this with some diced chopped veg, or sweeten and substantiate the base with chopped onion and garlic, but I like it just as it is, simple and huggy. To make this gluten free, simply replace the bread with gluten-free slices of your choice.

Pop the beans and carrots into a pan that will hold double their volume.

Pour over the tomatoes, add the garlic and the vegetable stock and sprinkle in the herbs. Bring to the boil, then reduce to a simmer and cook for 20 minutes until the beans start to soften.

Stir the bread pieces through the stew, then cook for a few minutes. Season with a little salt and pepper and add the lemon juice to taste. Serve hot.

This stew will keep in the fridge for 2 days, but it will thicken slightly, so add a splash more water if you are heating it from cold.

BUTTER BEAN & CIDER CASSOULET
VE

SERVES 4-6

3 tbsp garlic paste, or 1 whole head of garlic, finely chopped

200g frozen sliced onion, or 2 large onions, sliced

1 tbsp oil

2 x 200g tins of carrots, drained

a generous pinch of dried herbs

1 x 400g tin of cannellini beans, drained and rinsed

1 x 400g tin of butter beans, drained and rinsed

200ml cider

black pepper

½ tsp paprika

1.2 litres vegetable stock

1 tsp English mustard

1 tbsp vinegar or lemon juice

bread and greens, to serve

This soft, creamy cassoulet is a couple of tins of beans at their finest; simmered until gently collapsing, bolstered by a rich, slow-cooked flavour. In a nod to the traditional French version, I have added a smattering of paprika instead of the usual bacon pieces for a similar smoky flavour. I like to use cannellini beans with the butter beans but haricot, borlotti or baked beans (with the sauce rinsed off) work just as well. Leftovers can be frozen, and it also makes a tremendous pie filling.

First locate a large, wide pan – usually known as a sauté pan, but any pan will do. Toss the garlic and onions into the pan, add the oil and cook over a low heat, just to knock the raw, acerbic edge off your alliums. Cook for a couple of minutes until softened but not yet browning, then add the carrots too, along with the herbs. Give it all a stir and leave it on the heat.

Tip both lots of beans into the pan, followed shortly by the cider, a few pinches of pepper and the paprika. Bring the heat up to medium-high, and add a third of the stock. Allow the liquid to come to the boil, then reduce the heat to a simmer. Cook for 40 minutes, adding more stock as necessary to prevent it drying out, as the beans will thicken the sauce.

TIN CAN COOK

After 40 minutes, add the mustard and vinegar or lemon juice. Cook on a simmer for another 40 minutes, adding stock as required to prevent it drying out. Aware that this is a budget cooking book, I am at pains to point out that cooking on the hob is generally the least expensive way to cook (apart from a slow cooker, in which this recipe would work just fine with half the amount of stock) – so you can take more liberties with long cooking times on the hob than you could in the oven.

Remove from the heat completely, cover with a lid, foil or a large plate and let it sit for 40 minutes. It will continue to gently cook in its own retained heat and save you some money on your energy bills in the process.

Just before serving, heat through and stir well so it is evenly hot through, then serve – preferably with some bread and a pile of greens.

TIP

You can replace the cider with an equal volume of white wine if you have it knocking about.

BLACK BEAN DAAL

**SERVES 6–8
GENEROUSLY**

100g frozen sliced
onion, or 1 small
onion, diced

4 tbsp garlic paste, or
1 whole head of
garlic, chopped

1 tbsp oil

1 tbsp garam masala

1 tbsp curry powder

¼ tsp ground
cinnamon (optional)

½ tsp fennel seeds
(optional)

1 x 400g tin of black
beans, drained and
rinsed

1 x 400g tin of green
lentils, drained and
rinsed

1 x 400g tin of
chopped tomatoes

800ml chicken or
vegetable stock

100ml coconut milk

salt and pepper

This daal is based on one of my favourite recipes, from an Indian street food-inspired restaurant in London's Kings Cross, called Dishoom. They use black lentils and a 24-hour cooking time, as well as a splash of cream, to achieve their famously rich, creamy and decadent daal. This is a poor imitation of the original, which I have probably got all wrong, but it is still extremely good, and as a bonus it freezes really well, too. It's so easy to make this vegan if you swap chicken for vegetable stock.

Toss the onion into the largest saucepan you can find. This recipe makes a fairly generous amount of food, so you'll want a big vessel to cook it in! Then add the garlic to the pot. If using fresh garlic, the size doesn't matter so much here, as it has a long, slow cook to soften it; I like to leave mine fairly chunky, to find later on as sweet, hedonistic surprises.

Add the oil, garam masala, curry powder, cinnamon and fennel, if using, and set over a gentle heat. Cook together for around 5 minutes, stirring to coat the alliums in the spices.

Tip the black beans and green lentils into the pot. Add the tomatoes, and stir everything together. Cook for a further 5 minutes.

Add half the stock or the same 400ml water, and bring to the boil by turning up the heat. Reduce to a simmer as soon as it comes to the boil, stir well, and cook for 45 minutes, adding a little more stock or water occasionally if it thickens and looks like it is starting to dry out. Stir occasionally to stop the beans sticking and burning.

When the daal has been cooking for 45 minutes, stir through the coconut milk, and season with a few generous pinches of salt and pepper. It is ready to eat now, but if you can spare the time and the fuel, cooking it for a further half an hour really develops the flavours and takes this dish to a whole new level. If that sounds like a hassle, you can leave it to cool completely – it will continue to cook – for half an hour, then just blast it with a little more heat just before serving.

GOULASH
VE

SERVES 4

1 x 400g tin of kidney beans

1 x 400g tin of baked beans

100g frozen sliced onion or 1 small onion, finely sliced

1 fat clove of garlic, finely sliced, ½ tbsp garlic paste, or a generous shake of the dried stuff

4 tbsp oil

3 tsp paprika

1 x 400g tin of chopped tomatoes

1 vegetable stock cube

1 tsp sugar

To make this into a beef goulash, simply add a tin of corned beef at the same time as the kidney beans, and break it up with a wooden spoon. For a luxury version, rinse a tin of stewed steak and use that instead. No, I haven't lost my mind; it's a really neat trick for quickly adding some tender beef without having to cook it for hours on end. The bean version is, however, quite sufficient, and is my personal favourite.

Empty the kidney beans and the baked beans into a colander, and blast under cold running water to get rid of the tinned taste and the sauce from the baked beans. When well rinsed, set to one side.

Place the onion and garlic in a sauté or large non-stick frying pan with the oil and paprika and fry on a low heat until the onion is softened.

Add the chopped tomatoes, crumbled stock cube, sugar and half a tin (200ml) of water, and stir well. Simmer gently for 15 minutes until thickened and glossy. Tip in the colander of rinsed beans, stir to mix well and heat through for 10 minutes. Serve, devour, have seconds and enjoy!

TIN CAN COOK

CHILLI ROASTED CHICKPEAS
VE

SERVES 4 AS SNACKS

1 x 400g tin of chickpeas, drained

2 tbsp oil

a few pinches of salt

¼ tsp chilli, powder or dried chilli flakes

These chickpeas make for a tasty little snack, and once you have the hang of them, you can vary the flavours to use whatever you have to hand. A splash of lemon juice to taste works well, ¼ teaspoon ground cumin is nice, and a generous seasoning of salt and pepper is good, too. For a more substantial meal, use them to top a warm winter salad, or toss with scraps of meat and a loose tomato sauce for a quick dinner.

Preheat the oven to 180°C (fan 160°C/350°F/gas 4).

Give the chickpeas a good thorough rinse under the cold tap to get rid of the 'tinny' taste. (You can retain the liquor from the tin, see Tip on page 49.)

Tip the chickpeas into a mixing bowl and add the oil. Sprinkle over the salt and chilli and jostle the bowl gently to cover them all in oil and flavour. Tip them onto a baking tray or roasting tin – one with a lip around the edge, not a flat baking sheet, else they'll just roll off again!

Pop the tray into the oven for 30 minutes, removing it halfway through and shaking it gently to stop the chickpeas sticking and burning. Best served immediately.

BLACK BEAN & PEANUT STEW
VE

SERVES 2–4

100g frozen sliced
onion, or 1 small
onion, finely sliced

1 x 400g tin of black
beans, drained and
rinsed

1 tbsp oil

1 tsp paprika

1 tsp mixed dried
herbs (optional)

1 x 400g tin of
coconut milk

2 tbsp peanut butter,
smooth or crunchy

2 tbsp tomato purée
or ketchup

salt and pepper

100g green beans or
tinned peas

50g tinned or fresh
spinach (optional),
plus extra to serve

a dash of lemon
juice, fresh or bottled

plain white fluffy
rice, to serve

My original version of this dish contained chicken, but I have substituted it with black beans here. It makes for a more filling meal, and a cheaper one, too, as beans and pulses are generally far less expensive than meat and poultry. Dried beans work out even cheaper, but they require a degree of organisation to remember to soak them the evening before, or even to know what you will be eating in advance. I have never managed to be quite so organised, so it would be disingenuous of me to urge you all to do so, but if you are a meal-planning person, bear in mind that dried pulses may be less convenient than popping open a tin of pre-cooked ones, but they will save you money.

If you find black beans difficult to get hold of or they are not to your taste, you can use kidney beans, green lentils, or really, any bean will do. The cooking time given here is a minimum, not an absolute; as with any pulse-based stew, it will simply improve the longer it is cooked for. This recipe is also ideal for a slow cooker, if you have one. You can use tinned, fresh or frozen green beans or peas for this recipe.

Toss the onion into a large saucepan or shallow frying pan, then add the beans. Pour in the oil, and cook on a medium heat for a few minutes to take the raw edge off the onions, then add the paprika and mixed herbs (if using) and give it all a good stir.

Pour in 125ml water and the coconut milk, followed by the peanut butter and tomato purée or ketchup. Mix everything up and crank up the heat to full to bring it briefly to the boil – then reduce to a medium simmer again. Cook, stirring intermittently, for around 20 minutes, until the sauce has thickened and is a glossy reddish-brown colour.

Add the green beans or peas and spinach, if using, and cook for a further 5 minutes. Season to taste with salt, pepper and a dash of lemon, and serve. I serve mine with a pile of plain white fluffy rice and some extra greens, for good measure.

TIP
I like to throw a few dried chilli flakes all over my portion at the end, but they certainly aren't compulsory, especially if feeding little mouths.

RED LENTIL & MANDARIN CURRY
VE

SERVES 4

150g dried red lentils

1 tbsp ginger–garlic paste

1 tsp ground turmeric

1 tsp ground cumin

a pinch or two of dried chilli flakes, plus extra to serve (optional)

salt and pepper

1 x 300g tin of mandarins

1 x 400g tin of chopped tomatoes

The first time I stayed at a girlfriend's house, all she had in the cupboard was Diet Coke, tinned mandarins and a sticky patch of something ominous that was possibly once soy sauce. Her hob hadn't worked in over two years, and she stubbornly warned me not to try to change her.

Undeterred, over the course of our relationship I subtly snuck in the odd ingredient I could use to make microwaveable meals, a couple of spices to pep up salad dressings and a jar of ginger-garlic paste – 'just in case'. Turmeric and black pepper made it over the threshold as a cold remedy, and a tin of tomatoes for an emergency gazpacho that never materialized. I frequently joke with her that she keeps me grounded and keeps my recipes where they are meant to be – conjured up from dust and thin air and a couple of tins of nothing.

One week, left alone while she was out on a jolly, and armed with a YouTube video, a dogbone wrench, a Phillips screwdriver and a mission, I fixed the damn hob. And one cold winter night, faced with just a literal handful of stashed ingredients and disbelieving cries of 'what on earth could you make with what's in MY cupboard?', I threw this together.

Pop the lentils into a saucepan that will easily hold double their volume, and cover with water. Do not salt the water as the lentils will seize and harden. Bring to the boil and reduce to a vigorous simmer for around 10 minutes, then drain and thoroughly rinse to get rid of the greyish scum that will have risen to the surface. Tip them back into the pan and return it to the heat.

Add the ginger-garlic paste (or finely chopped fresh ginger and garlic if you don't have any, but I swear by this as a quick cheap fix – you can find jars of it in the World Foods aisle in the supermarket). Add the spices – turmeric, cumin and chilli – and a pinch of salt and a few pinches of pepper, and give it all a good stir. Crank the heat back up high.

Drain the mandarins, reserving the juice (see Tip). Sling the mandarins into the pan, and add the tomatoes. Cook the lot for a further 20 minutes or longer – using lentils makes this more like a daal, and the longer cook lends itself to softer, swollen lentils with a comforting, creamy texture.

Serve hot with extra chilli to taste – in my small household we all have a wildly varying tolerance to heat, so I put a smattering in the curry and leave a small dish of chilli flakes in residence on the table for the bolder members to use with abandon.

TIP
Some brands of tinned mandarins come in orange juice, which I neck greedily, and some come in a sticky-sweet syrup, which I put in a jar in the fridge to use in a salad dressing or cake.

MUSHROOM, LENTIL & BEER PIE
VE

SERVES 6

FOR THE FILLING

1 x 390g tin of green
or brown lentils

100g frozen sliced
onion or 1 small
onion, finely sliced

2 tbsp garlic paste or
6 fat cloves of garlic,
chopped

2 tbsp flour, plus
extra for dusting

2 tbsp oil

250ml vegan beer

1 veg stock cube

2 tbsp tomato
ketchup or purée

200g tinned carrots,
diced or sliced

400g mushrooms,
diced or sliced

1 tbsp meat-style
gravy granules

1 tsp lemon juice

FOR THE PASTRY

300g ready-made
shortcrust pastry

1 tbsp oil, to glaze

This pie came about because, firstly, I adore pie. It was my pregnancy craving, some years ago now; steak pie followed by cherry or apple pie. I would buy packets of Mr Kipling and polish them off by the half dozen. Something about the crumbling, yielding collapse of the pastry, the hot-or-cold, sweet-or-savoury, the lingering lubrication, satiation, of a layer of fat and gravy disappearing down my greedy gullet. I make a pie most weeks, more so since cooking vegan food than ever before. This particular pie came from a longing for something 'meaty', but not meat, of course. A hearty, wholesome, dark and brooding pie with base and top that would fool even the hardiest of carnivores. Fortunately most ready-made pastry is vegan, as are a very well-known brand of gravy granules.

First pop the lentils into a saucepan that will easily hold three times their volume. Cover with cold water, but do not salt them or they will seize and harden. Bring to the boil at the back of the stove, where they can be forgotten for a while. Reduce to a simmer and roundly ignore them for around half an hour, only interfering should they start to dry out a little, then just add a splash of water.

In a separate pan over a low heat, add the onion and garlic. Stir in the flour and oil – it will look dreadful, but give it a chance – and cook, mixing well to a rough, chunky paste. Add a splash of the beer, which will fizz pleasantly, and mix to loosen it. Add a splash more, mix, splash, mix, until half of the beer is combined. Set the other half to one side. Crumble in the stock cube, then squeeze in the ketchup, and mix well. Add the carrots and mushrooms to the pot. Bring everything to the boil, then reduce to a simmer, until the lentils behind them on the stove have softened.

When the lentils have cooked and the pie filling is glossy and unctuous and reduced in volume, it is time to combine the two. Drain the lentils and rinse thoroughly to get rid of any residual white scum, then tip them into the pan with the mushrooms and beer. Mix them together well – you may find you need to add a little more beer to the mixture, so do. Add the gravy granules and mix well, bearing in mind that they will thicken the liquid when cooked, so it can afford to be a little runny at this stage. Finish with a dash of lemon to brighten it, as the beer can be quite a heavy, mouth-filling flavour.

At this point, if you are cooking the pie now, turn your oven on to 180°C (fan 160°C/350°F/gas 4) and make sure that there is a shelf in the middle of it for best results.

→

Roll out your pastry on a lightly floured surface. Lightly grease a pie tin or similar receptacle – I find a 900g loaf tin makes a very pleasing pie in an emergency, and a Victoria sponge tin creates a thinner one with a good pastry-to-filling ratio. Any leftover filling can always be frozen to make future pies, or eaten as a casserole, so the size of your tin is not prescriptive. Lay the pastry carefully in the tin, pressing it gently into the corners. The weight of the filling will do the rest for you.

Spoon in the filling, working your way from the outside to the middle, and gradually so as not to overbear and thus tear your precious pastry. Fill it to the top – don't be shy – underfilled pies have their own circle in Hell in my books.

Now make the top. I am naturally incompetent at delicate tasks, my rough-hewn hands more suited to heaving large objects around, fiddling in u-bends and smashing together flatpack furniture than delicately fiddling with pastry, and so, as with many things, I have found a method that is both simple and idiot-proof, and looks astounding. I make my pie crusts with tessellated or overlaying cookie-cutter shapes, the effect of which is beautiful and elicits squeals of delight from guests of all ages. I highly recommend it – and if the pieces overlap, there is more pastry per mouthful, which can only be a glorious thing. Roll out your excess pastry to around 4mm thick. Take a cookie cutter of your choice, or if you live in a household without small children, you can use a small glass for the same effect. Cut circles of pastry and carefully lay them on top of the pie – it doesn't matter if there are gaps, in fact, they rather pleasingly get sticky with caramelized gravy, so embrace them. Start from the outside and work your way in, until the pie is covered or all the pastry is used up.

Glaze with a little oil. Place it in the oven and bake for 40 minutes, or until the pastry is golden. You may wish to re-glaze halfway through, for extra sheen. I did, but then this is my living, and I need to tempt you here any way I can.

And serve. I find this quite sufficient on its own, my excuse for no sides being that it contains a hefty dose of our 5-a-day (onion, mushroom, tomato, carrot, lentils) and because in our household, we like pie.

POTATOES

PATATAS BRAVAS
VE

SERVES 2

100ml cooking oil (you may not use all of it)

1 tsp dried chilli flakes

1 tsp paprika

500g drained tinned potatoes

salt and pepper

A classic Spanish tapas recipe, Patatas Bravas is usually made with fresh potatoes rather than tinned ones. I have made this recipe several times as part of a dinner party for guests, or to warm myself on a cold winter night, and it may be that I am used to tinned spuds by now but I genuinely didn't feel this was any the lesser for using them. Quick, simple and filling – with a kick!

First make your chilli oil. If you have a small bullet blender, pop the oil, chilli and paprika in it and blend quickly to combine. This makes a rather potent and very hot chilli oil, which adds a fiery kick to the potatoes. Traditional recipes make their own chilli oil by steeping dried chillies in bottles of oil for weeks on end, but I don't generally plan my dinners that far in advance, so this is a simple trick I use instead.

Carefully halve the potatoes and pop them into a large, shallow, non-stick saucepan. Pour half the chilli oil into the pan and bring to a medium heat. Cook for around 15 minutes, turning every now and then, until they are golden brown at the edges. You may need to add more oil; not all potatoes are created equal.

To serve, season with a little salt and pepper. Best enjoyed hot, but they make a potato salad with attitude if allowed to cool!

WARM POTATO SALAD WITH ANCHOVY MAYO

SERVES 24,
DEPENDING ON
APPETITE

1 x 50g tin of
anchovies, drained

100g mayonnaise

1 tbsp lemon juice

500g drained tinned
potatoes, cut in half

I first had anchovy mayonnaise at Hawksmoor in Seven Dials, Covent Garden, with the food writer and now dearly beloved friend, Xanthe Clay. I stored it in the back burner of my imagination, and here is my admittedly slovenly and poorer version of it, knocked together with tins rather than lovingly handmade with egg yolks and olive oil. I can only apologise; I am rather fond of bastardizing brilliant ideas, and this is no exception.

First make your anchovy mayonnaise, or rather, 'combine' it, as I'm sure food purists would have a thing or two to say about me describing this as 'making' anything. Tip the anchovies and mayo into a small blender and pulse a few times until it turns a soft mink colour. If you don't have a small blender, you can do this by hand, but it is a little work – finely chop the anchovies and place them in a larger-than-you-think mixing bowl. You'll need the extra room to really bash them about. Add the mayo and, using a fork, beat seven shades of something out of them until everything is combined.

Spoon the anchovy mayo into a clean jar with a lid and fold in the lemon juice gently – you may not need all of the mayo for this recipe, and it's lovely with chips!

Pop the potatoes into a pan of water and bring to the boil, then immediately reduce to a simmer. Cook for 4 minutes until everything is warmed through.

Remove from the heat and drain thoroughly. Spoon over the anchovy mayonnaise and gently stir or shake the warm potatoes to coat them. Serve immediately warm, or chilled.

SPEEDY BUBBLE

SERVES 2-4

500g drained, tinned potatoes

200g drained, tinned carrots

100g drained, tinned spinach

1 egg (not essential, you can replace with an extra tablespoon of flour if you are vegan)

3–4 tbsp flour

1 tbsp garlic paste, or 2 fat cloves of garlic, crushed

¼ tsp mustard

salt and pepper

oil, for frying

Bubble and squeak is the traditional Monday morning mashup of the Sunday roast, but sometimes I fancy it when there isn't a spare roast dinner laying about. The tinned veg here is unorthodox but actually makes for an easier mashing experience, so faster bubble! Tinned spinach can be a little grim in any significant quantity – so don't be tempted to sling the lot in, make the leftovers into a soup with a lot, and I mean a lot, of garlic and lemon juice and stock.

Add the potatoes and carrots to a large saucepan and cover with water. Bring to the boil over a medium heat then reduce to a simmer for 10 minutes to soften them up real good. Drain and tip into a mixing bowl.

Drain the spinach, if necessary, and add to the pan, stirring well to form an ominously green mush. Beat in an egg, if using, and add enough flour to stiffen the mixture. I like to add a dash of garlic paste and a little mustard here, and some salt and pepper. Cover and chill the mixture for 30 minutes to firm it up.

Once chilled, shape into small round patties. Heat a little oil in a frying pan over a medium heat and cook the patties for 3–4 minutes on either side. Serve hot.

MONSTER MASH

SERVES 2 AS A SIDE DISH

salt

500g drained and rinsed tinned potatoes

a splash of milk (plant-based milk is fine if you're that way inclined)

a knob of butter or margarine or a splash of oil

400g drained, tinned spinach

Originally thrown together as a way to encourage my son to eat his greens when he started to go through a fussy stage, this bright little number is a tasty accompaniment to many of the stews and casseroles in this book. For a more grown-up palate, add a dash of mustard or garlic.

Bring a pan of slightly salted water to the boil. Pop in the potatoes, reduce the heat to a simmer and cook for around 15 minutes, until the potatoes are super soft. They will already be cooked, so this is just a softening-up exercise to make them mashable.

When the potatoes are soft, drain them well. Add a splash of milk and the butter, margarine or oil, and mash well with a fork or masher, until smooth. Add the spinach, a heaped spoon at a time, until it is the desired shade of green. When I first made this, I blended the spinach to a paste and stirred it through to disguise it, then once my son acquired the taste for it, I stopped bothering and just stirred it through whole.

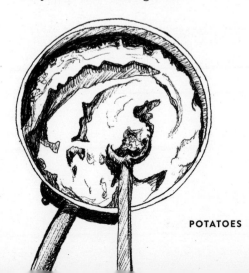

RED MUSHROOM & POTATO CURRY
VE

SERVES 2–4,
DEPENDING ON
APPETITE

100g frozen sliced
onion or 1 small
onion, finely sliced

1 tbsp garlic paste, or
4 cloves of garlic,
finely sliced

a small piece of fresh
root ginger, roughly
chopped

¼ tsp dried chilli
flakes

50g tomato purée

200ml coconut milk

400g mushrooms,
tinned, frozen or
fresh, cut in half

oil, for frying

salt

400g tinned potatoes

1 tsp lemon juice

This hot and spicy little number is a favourite in my household for dealing with the dreaded cold and flu, or when someone's feeling a little run down. The combination of garlic, ginger, chilli, tomatoes and a kick of citrus is a feisty relief for the symptoms of even the most grim winter germs. I make a double batch of the paste and pop it in the freezer for future use. Of course, you can use a jar of shop-bought curry paste if you are feeling really rough; I've been there and I absolutely sympathize. I blitz mine in a blender to get the paste super smooth, but it's not essential, you can just throw it all in a pan for a similar effect, just with a little extra texture.

I sometimes like to pad this out with a finely chopped cabbage or a handful of frozen spinach or peas stirred through 5 minutes before the end.

Make the curry paste by tossing the onion, garlic and ginger into a blender, along with the chilli, tomato puree and 100ml of the coconut milk. Blitz it to a rough paste and set to one side.

Toss the mushrooms into a large pan with a dash of oil and a pinch of salt. Cook over a medium heat to gently brown the outsides for a few minutes, then tip in the curry paste, add the remaining coconut milk, and the potatoes, and stir well. Bring to a boil then reduce to a simmer and cook for 20 minutes, until the mushrooms have softened and the curry paste has thickened slightly. Stir through the lemon juice and serve.

PASTA

NO-COOK PASTA

SERVES 1

a handful of dried pasta shapes

a pinch of salt

your topping of choice (see recipe introduction)

Here I am going to share a simple trick that changed my life. I spend most of my time with a nine-year-old boy and a small ginger cat, but sometimes I find myself on my own, touring for work, and without any cooking facilities with which to feed myself. I learned to keep small sachets of Marmite in my work bag, a shaker of dried cheese and a small freezerbag of pasta, and now, no matter where I am, as long as I have a kettle and a mug I have dinner. This also works for evenings where depression strikes and I don't have the energy to drag myself to the cooker and rustle up something restaurant-worthy. You can stir anything you like through it, such as grated mixed vegetables, sweetcorn and cheese, salmon paste – the combinations are limitless. You may never boil a pan for pasta for one again.

First pop the pasta into the largest mug you can find. It should ideally fill the mug halfway.

Boil the kettle and pour the boiling water over the pasta, about 1cm from the top of the mug. Add a pinch of salt and give it a careful stir. Quickly place a saucer or bowl on top of the mug to trap in the heat. Leave it to stand for 10 minutes.

After 10 minutes, the pasta should be cooked and swollen and soft. If it isn't, you can top it back up with boiling water and repeat for a few more minutes, or pop it in the microwave for 2 minutes (if you have one to hand!).

Drain any excess water and stir through your topping of choice, and enjoy.

TIN CAN COOK

PASTA E FAGIOLI (PASTA & BEANS)
VE

SERVES 4

1 x 400g tin of white beans (cannellini or borlotti), drained and rinsed

200g tinned, chopped tomatoes or 2 tbsp tomato purée

500ml vegetable stock

handful of fresh chopped herbs of your choice

6–12 cloves of garlic, depending on how bold you are

160g small pasta shapes – any will do

The much-beloved godfather of Italian cookery, Antonio Carluccio, once described *pasta e fagioli* as 'the best-known peasant dish in Italy, but smart enough for posh restaurant menus. For me it is the benchmark of a good chef; because it is so simple, it must be perfect.' The restaurant versions use dried beans, soaked and cooked for hours, and fresh tomatoes. This simplification uses, as befits the title of the book, tins of both. Some renditions have carrots added, and of course you may sling in a tin of those too, if you like.

Tip the beans into a medium or large saucepan. Pour over the tinned tomatoes or purée and the stock. Add the herbs, and peel and toss in the garlic cloves. Cook for 30 minutes over a medium heat to really soften the beans and get them deliciously creamy. You may need to add an extra splash of water, depending on how fierce your hob is – just make sure the pan doesn't dry out as you will need to cook the pasta in it later.

After 30 minutes, add the pasta and a little extra water to cover it. Cook for a further 10 minutes (pasta cooked in sauce takes a few minutes longer than when cooked in water alone), and serve.

TIP

In Italy it is traditional to serve soups warm, not piping hot, but this is a rule I often flout! In this case, however, eating it warm allows the flavour to develop more and elevates this humble meal to something quite spectacular. That's my opinion, anyway, which you are free to entirely disregard.

PASTA E CECI
(PASTA & CHICKPEAS)

1 x 400g tin of chickpeas, drained and rinsed

6 cloves of garlic, peeled, or 2 tbsp garlic paste

vegetable stock cube dissolved in 700ml boiling water

1 x 400g tin of chopped tomatoes

1 tsp vinegar

1 tbsp oil or 15g butter

½ tsp mixed dried herbs

salt and pepper

1 x 400g tin of spaghetti hoops

a pinch of chilli powder or dried chilli flakes (optional)

Pasta and chickpeas is a classic Roman dish, and I have upped the 'tin factor' on this version by making it with tinned spaghetti hoops because, why on earth not? Tinned spaghetti is pre-cooked and very very soft, so it needs little more than a gentle warm through at the end.

This recipe may look a little impetuous, or at the very least unappetizing, but it is so much more than the sum of its parts, I promise you.

Tip the chickpeas into a medium saucepan and add the garlic cloves – whole is fine as they will be cooking for quite some time, so will end up soft and sweet rather than raw and terrifying – or use paste. Add the stock (or just use 700ml water) and bring to a boil, then reduce to a simmer. Cook for 40 minutes to make the chickpeas super soft and squishy.

Pour over the tomatoes and add the vinegar, oil or butter, herbs and a pinch of salt and a good grinding of pepper, then cook for a further 10 minutes.

Tip the spaghetti hoops into a sieve or colander and rinse very slowly and gently to get rid of as much of the sticky orange sauce as possible. I must admit I omit this step as I don't mind the sauce and like the sweetness it adds, but if I were cooking it for someone else I would rinse it off! Add the hoops to the pan and warm through for 2 minutes, stirring carefully, then serve with a grinding of pepper and some chilli on top, if you like.

TUNA, SWEETCORN & MUSHROOM PASTA

SERVES 4

200g dried pasta shapes

1 x 400g tin of mushroom soup

1 x 320g tin of sweetcorn (a smaller one will do), drained

1 x 160g tin of tuna, or 2 if you can spare them, drained

salt and pepper

grated cheese (if you have it, no worries if you don't), to serve

One of my earliest childhood memories of my mum cooking was watching her tip pasta into an ovenproof dish and cover it with a can of soup. She would then refill the soup tin twice with water, stir it in, and pop the dish in the oven. What emerged was nothing short of a miracle. Sometimes it would be doused in cheese, but my parents were not well-off and liked to remind me that cheese was expensive, usually as they caught me slicing chunks of it for myself as a contraband snack. My dad's version was a tin of tomatoes instead of soup, so tightly packed it resembled a bright-red breeze block, that he would slice into slabs, silently daring us to conquer the mountain of carbs before us.

Refilling a tin with water to loosen the soup and provide enough liquid for the pasta to cook in is a fantastic idea, and works with pretty much any soup you fancy. Here I have used a classic combination of tinned tuna and mushroom soup – far more delicious than it sounds – and this one makes a creamy, soupy pasta with not a breeze block in sight. Make double if you like, as this freezes really well.

First grab a large saucepan. Add the pasta. Pour over the soup, then fill the soup tin with water and add that too. Refill the tin again with water and stand it to one side; you'll need it later.

Bring to the boil and reduce to a simmer, then cook for 10–12 minutes, adding more water as you need to. Stir it occasionally to stop it sticking to the bottom of the pan and burning. Keep checking to see if the pasta is cooked – pasta cooked in sauce instead of plain water does tend to take a little longer than the packet instructions specify; it's not an exact science, but I tend to multiply the given time by 1.5 and it generally works out okay.

Towards the end of the cooking time, when the pasta is soft and the sauce is thick and soupy, tip in the sweetcorn. Add the tuna and stir it through. Taste it, and season with salt and pepper if you want to. I happen to like a generous kick of pepper in pretty much anything, and it certainly goes well here.

Serve in bowls, as it is comfortingly sloppy. Top with cheese if you have it, but it's just fine without.

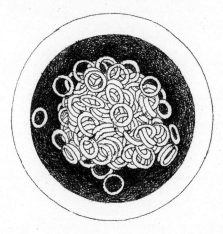

ABSOLUTELY BASIC PUTTANESCA

SERVES 2 (WITH LEFTOVER SAUCE)

100g tomato purée

2 x 50g tins of anchovies in olive oil

pepper

a dash of lemon juice

a pinch of dried chilli flakes or powder

100g pasta shapes

Puttanesca is a store-cupboard spaghetti dish that's traditionally made from whatever is to hand; key elements include tomatoes, anchovies, chilli and olives, and whatever else takes your fancy. Jamie Oliver adds tuna to his, Nigella capers; I have dispensed with all of the additions and simply thrown this one in a pan.

This recipe makes enough sauce for around eight portions; I freeze leftovers in an ice cube tray or in freezer bags for future use. It only improves with time, too, so do make it ahead and freeze it!

Pop the purée, anchovies and oil, a good grinding of pepper, the lemon juice and chilli in a saucepan with 300ml water. Cook for 20 minutes over a medium heat. Pour some of the sauce into a jar, leaving a quarter to a third in the pan.

Add the pasta to the pan and cook for 10 minutes more or until the pasta cooks, adding a splash of water, if required. That's it, really. It's called Absolutely Basic for a reason!

CONCHIGLIE WITH BROAD BEANS & ARTICHOKES

V

SERVES 2

salt and pepper

200g conchiglie pasta

1 x 300g tin of broad beans, drained

50g sliced artichokes in oil, drained

1 tbsp garlic paste or 2 fat cloves of garlic, crushed

a dash of white wine (optional)

2 tbsp oil

a handful of fresh mint, chopped

1 tbsp lemon juice

grated hard strong cheese, to serve (optional)

One of my favourite cookery manuals is an obscure and beautiful number. *The Geometry of Pasta*, by chef Jacob Kenedy and designer Caz Hildebrand, appeals both to my autistic obsessive nature and my love of carbs. It pairs 100 pasta sauce recipes with their perfect pasta shape, each deliberately designed to delicately enhance the other. When I first conceived of this recipe, I placed a tin of broad beans next to a jar of sliced artichokes, guiding them towards the 'pasta' chapter in my head. 'What would Jacob do?' I muttered to myself, and went to fetch the book. He pairs broad beans with conchiglie, the deep shell of the latter acting as a nest for the former. So, without hesitation, conchiglie it is. Enjoy.

Bring a large pan of salted water to the boil, and tip in the pasta. You'll want more salt than you think; around 1 tablespoon per 200g of pasta is my rule of thumb, but I do admit that after years in this game, my palate leans towards salinity. Reduce the heat to a simmer and cook for 8 minutes, keeping an eye on the pasta so it doesn't stick or burn.

Grab a separate pan, ideally a wide, shallow non-stick one. Tip in the broad beans along with the artichokes, garlic, wine (if using), oil, mint, salt and pepper. Bring to a medium heat and cook, stirring intermittently to combine everything.

When the pasta is cooked, drain it and pop it back into the pan. Tip in the contents of the other pan. Season again with pepper, and mix vigorously to coat the pasta in the beans and greens. Serve immediately, with the lemon juice, and some hard cheese grated over, if you like.

ANELLINI CON CACIO E PEPE (SPAGHETTI HOOPS WITH CHEESE & PEPPER)

V

SERVES 1

1 x 400g tin of spaghetti hoops

15g butter or 1 tbsp oil

hard strong cheese, grated

pinch of black pepper

This recipe came about on a miserable evening; I was out of sorts, grumpy and didn't want to cook for myself, let alone delve into my imagination and create something wonderful. It happens here and there, and I have learned over the years that the best way to keep the black dog at bay is by feeding him carbs and cheese and going to bed satiated with a book to escape into. But this particular evening, I didn't even have the emotional energy to boil a pan for pasta. I didn't want to. Life gets us like that sometimes, and I'm hoping that this recipe will come in handy for those of you who find yourselves needing a little swift self-care every now and then.

Cacio e pepe is one of my favourite dishes; in its true form, it's soft spaghetti tossed in butter or olive oil, with Parmesan or Grana Padano finely grated in, and a hefty dose of black pepper. I make that version often, but this is a sloppy stand-in, that's about 95 per cent as good as the original, with 5 per cent of the work. And it's ready in 2 minutes, too.

Tip the spaghetti hoops into a sieve and gently rinse them to get rid of the tomato sauce. Transfer to a microwave-proof bowl. Microwave on full power for 90 seconds. Remove, stir and microwave for 30 seconds more. If you don't have a microwave, heat through gently and quickly on the hob – they will fall apart a little but will still be delicious!

Remove the pasta from the microwave and add the butter or oil, cheese and a pinch of pepper. Stir through. Enjoy immediately. Repeat as desired.

PASTA WITH A
LEMONY OLIVE TAPENADE
VE

SERVES 2

120g stoned black olives

2 tbsp oil

1 tbsp lemon juice or wine vinegar

salt and pepper

120g spaghetti or linguine

a pinch of dried chilli flakes (optional)

Ooh, I hear you say, olives! I love an olive, and again, they are wrongly maligned as being some kind of fancy foodstuff, when at the time of writing this they are 75p for a 330g tin in the local supermarket. Seventy-five pence! And a little goes a long way; you only need a handful of olives for this recipe, as their pungent salty taste packs quite a bang for your buck.

Classic black olive tapenade uses capers and anchovies; I've omitted them here because they're not really essential, but if you happen to have anchovies kicking about (they're in a few recipes in this book!), then one or two wouldn't go amiss – but reduce the salt you add, as it's there to compensate for their absence.

First finely pulverize your olives – either by hand on a wooden board with a very sharp knife, or in a small blender. If using a blender please, please make sure your olives have already been de-stoned; for reasons I will never quite understand, market forces dictate that cheaper olives tend to come with the fiddly work already done for you, while the fancier varieties have stones intact. I prefer the cheaper ones, both for cooking and for my wallet, but do check, as a rogue olive stone will irreparably damage the blades of your blender.

Scrape the olive paste into a small bowl, and add the oil, lemon juice and salt and pepper. Beat well with a fork to thoroughly combine.

Bring a pan of water to the boil and add your spaghetti – I break mine in half to make it easier and so it all fits in the pan without singed edges as inevitably I get distracted sometimes and babysitting spaghetti is not high on my priorities list. Simmer for 7–8 minutes until cooked to your liking.

Drain the pasta and tip back into the pan. Toss with the olive purée and add the chilli and/or more black pepper, and serve.

CANNELLINI BEURRE BLANC

SERVES 2

FOR THE BEANS AND PASTA

1 x 400g tin of cannellini beans or haricot beans, drained and rinsed

800ml vegetable or chicken stock

120g small pasta shapes

pepper

FOR THE BEURRE BLANC

4 tbsp white wine or cider

4 tbsp white wine vinegar or cider vinegar

1 tbsp garlic paste or 2 fat cloves of garlic, finely chopped

25g butter

I have very little time for the notion that some foods are 'not for poorer people' – it is a criticism I have come up against time and again, whether it is kale pesto irritating the commentariat at the *Daily Mail*, or a slosh of £2.50 table wine in a risotto, there is a frankly hideous misconception that good food is for the 'deserving', with the parameters of who deserves exactly what seemingly set by those who have never had a tenner in their pocket to last a week. Sometimes, when testing new recipes, I have a moment of hesitation, wondering how to frame it to reduce the petty background chatter around what I consider to be 'food for everyone'. And then I carry on.

This was one such recipe. An unctuous and subtly powerful sauce reduced to a thick, provocative shroud for slow-cooked cannellini beans and a scant handful of pasta. It would sit proudly on any hifalutin restaurant menu, but its main ingredient is a tin of beans and a slug of vinegar. You can use wine or cider for the sauce; and only a few tablespoons of each. I make this for myself often, in varying guises; and once you have the knack for it, I'm sure you will too. And politics be damned; I want to live in a world where everyone should be able to put a beurre blanc on the table without hesitation.

Pop the beans into a large saucepan that will easily hold three times their volume; for you will be adding pasta to this later. Cover with the stock, and bring to the boil. Reduce to a simmer for 20 minutes; the longer the cooking time, the softer and creamier the beans will be.

While the beans are cooking, make the beurre blanc in a separate small pan. Combine all of the ingredients and cook on a low–medium heat, for 15 minutes, to reduce the volume and combine the fat and acid together. You will need to keep an eye on this and stir it fairly continuously, as I have burned and lost many a beurre blanc sauce through a moment's distraction. Turn off the heat and allow the beurre blanc to settle.

When the beans have cooked for 20 minutes, add the pasta. Cook the pasta for 10 minutes, or until soft, then combine with the beurre blanc sauce. Season generously with pepper, and enjoy.

FISH

LEMON-ROASTED SARDINES

SERVES 2

1 lemon or lime, thinly sliced

2 x 90g tins of sardines in oil

salt and pepper

I first made this recipe for friends on holiday; we were staying in Spain and the nearest supermarket had an entire aisle of tinned fish. Sardines were 1 euro for three tins, and we lived off them all week. Initially my housemates were sceptical at my enthusiasm for feeding them tinned fish all week; by the end of the first dinner-time, there wasn't a scrap left and everyone requested them again. They're simple, barely any effort, but a real showstopper if you have friends for tea. If you don't, just pop them on toast or toss through pasta with a little tomato sauce for a quick and easy meal.

First preheat your oven to 190°C (fan 170°C/375°F/gas 5).

Next, lay your lemon or lime slices in the bottom of a small roasting dish, to cover it if possible.

Open the tins of sardines, and drain the oil into a small jar. You can pop this into the fridge and keep it for 2 weeks to cook something fishy in, like fishcakes, or anything you don't mind having a slightly umami background taste.

Using a fork or a small sharp knife, gently remove the sardines one by one and lay them on the lemon slices, keeping them as whole as you can manage.

Season with a little salt and pepper, and pop the dish into the oven for 30 minutes to roast. The whole dish can be eaten, including the lemon slices, which will be soft, tart, sweet and a perfect companion to the salty strong sardines.

CATALAN-STYLE FISH STEW

SERVES 4-6

100g frozen sliced onion or 1 small onion, finely sliced

200g drained, tinned carrots, cut in half

500g drained, tinned potatoes, cut in half

1 tbsp oil

salt and pepper

1 tsp hot paprika

a pinch of dried mixed herbs

2 tbsp garlic paste, or 4 cloves of garlic, peeled but left whole

1 x 400g tin of chopped tomatoes

125ml white wine or beer (optional)

1 x 400g tin of white beans, drained and rinsed

2 x 90g tins of sardines in oil

a dash of lemon juice

This recipe is a very pared-down version of a Catalan classic; in place of chorizo, I have added a dose of paprika and garlic to give the same flavours for less money. I would usually use 125ml each of water and white wine or light beer, but vary the proportions according to what you have available and can afford. The traditional recipe uses a variety of shellfish and freshwater fish; I have plumped for the humble tinned sardine, making this almost a store-cupboard recipe, and one that can be rustled up in a pinch. You can use tinned cockles, mussels, or white fish fillets, if you prefer.

Toss the onion, carrots and potatoes into a large saucepan. Add the oil and a pinch of salt and cook for a few minutes over a low heat to soften. Add the paprika and mixed herbs. Add the garlic and season with a pinch of salt and a little pepper.

Pour over the tin of tomatoes and add 125ml water and the wine or beer, if using, or 250ml water. Add the beans to the pot. Turn up the heat and cook for 20 minutes until the onion and garlic have softened and the beans are starting to fall apart a little.

In a separate pan, gently heat a little oil from the sardine tins. Carefully lift each sardine from the tin, slowly and delicately so as not to break them. Place in the pan and turn the heat up high to crisp the skin. Cook for 2–3 minutes then turn over and cook for 2–3 minutes more.

Spoon the stew into bowls, and top each with some crisp sardines. Dress with a dash of lemon juice and a little pepper, and enjoy.

BEER-BATTERED SARDINES

SERVES 2-3

100g plain flour, plus 4 tbsp

1 egg

300ml light-coloured beer

black pepper

oil, for cooking

2 x 90g tins of sardines in oil

lemon juice, to serve

Most tinned sardines have soft-enough bones to be able to eat them, but do take care to examine them before you cook them; and lift out any larger bones with a small sharp knife or tweezers if they trouble you. That said, this recipe is a good way of getting otherwise-strong sardines into my young son, although I may be setting him up for an early taste for beer, which could come back to haunt us! When cooking with hot oil, keep your eyes on it at all times and do not leave the pan unattended.

First make up your batter. In a large bowl, beat together 100g of the flour with the egg and a little beer to form a smooth paste. I find it easiest to use a fork for this, to prevent lumps forming, but a wooden spoon works too

Thin the batter with a little more beer, adding it gradually until the batter is smooth and runny. If you have any stubborn lumps, simply strain them out through a sieve; life is too short to worry about such things.

Pour the batter into a small bowl, season with black pepper and pop it into the fridge for at least an hour to chill.

Grab a small saucepan – deep frying in a shallow pan is far less terrifying than a huge rolling vat of oil raging on your back burner. Add 7cm of oil to the pan, and pop on a medium heat for a few minutes, until small bubbles start to drift to the surface. Drop half a teaspoon of batter into the pan; if it instantly floats and sizzles, you're good to go. If it goes pale and flooby, wait a minute and try again.

Open the sardines, drain them and pop them in a mixing bowl. Add the 4 tablespoons of flour and gently – gently – shake the bowl from side to side to coat them in flour. This helps the batter stick.

Carefully place a sardine into the bowl of batter, and coat in batter. Lift it out with a slotted spoon and lower it into the oil. Repeat for another sardine, and then another one, making sure your pan doesn't get too crowded, you can do these in batches if you need to. Turn the heat down to low when the sardines go in to stop the oil from catching and burning – many a kitchen fire has been started by deep frying, so please, please be careful, and if the pan starts to smoke, remove it from the heat IMMEDIATELY and leave it somewhere safe to cool down. DO NOT POUR COLD WATER ON IT. If the pan of oil starts to smoke, I wrap a soaking wet tea towel around the handle and over the top and march it outside, and place it down on the concrete driveway, but I am extraordinarily fire-conscious, what with having been in the actual fire service for a few years. Anyway. Back to the sardines.

Line a mixing bowl with kitchen paper or a clean tea towel, or place them on a plate if you don't have a mixing bowl to hand. Clean your slotted spoon, you'll need it again in a second.

When the sardines are cooked, remove with that slotted spoon and place carefully on the paper or tea towel. Repeat with as many sardines as you have. Top with lemon juice and serve hot, and immediately.

COCKLE SPAGHETTI

SERVES 2

1 large onion, diced, or 100g frozen sliced onion

1 tbsp oil

salt and pepper

1 x 400g tin of chopped tomatoes

a pinch of dried chilli flakes or chilli powder

1 tbsp garlic paste

180g spaghetti

150g drained pickled cockles in vinegar

The vinegar that the cockles are cooked in makes for a pleasantly tangy pasta sauce. Pickled mussels also work well here, if you can find them.

Put the onion in a medium saucepan with the oil and a pinch of salt, and cook on a low heat for 5 minutes until it starts to soften. Pour over the tomatoes, and add the chilli and garlic, and cook for 15 minutes over a medium heat to start to reduce the tomatoes down to a thick, glossy sauce.

Bring a separate pan of water to the boil. Salt it and add the spaghetti, and cook according to the packet instructions, around 8–10 minutes.

When the spaghetti is cooked, turn off the heat. Add the cockles to the pasta sauce. Drain the spaghetti and serve it with the sauce dolloped on top. Finish with black pepper, if you like.

SIMPLER CRABBY PASTA

SERVES 2

salt and pepper

160g pasta

100g frozen sliced onion or 1 small onion, finely sliced

1 tbsp cooking oil

1 tbsp lemon juice

75g crab or salmon paste

100ml milk (UHT will do fine)

a pinch of dried chilli flakes or chilli powder, to serve

This is a variation of the third most popular recipe on my website, which has at the time of writing surpassed 32 million visitors. I include this information because when I first posted it, it was met with scorn and disbelief from the upper echelons of the cooking world, but my readers loved it for its simplicity and flavour. You can judge for yourself! You can use crab paste or salmon paste here; either works, and I have also made it with chicken paste and tinned sweetcorn, too.

First bring a medium saucepan of water to the boil. Salt it, and add the pasta. Reduce the heat to a simmer and allow the pasta to cook for 8–10 minutes, according to the packet instructions.

Meanwhile, plonk the onion into a large, shallow pan, add the oil, salt and pepper, and lemon juice, and cook over a medium heat, to soften. Stir in the crab or salmon paste, and thin with a splash of milk, adding the milk slowly to make a creamy sauce.

When the pasta is cooked, remove it from the heat and drain it thoroughly. Tip the pasta into the sauce. Stir quickly to combine it and coat the pasta, and serve sprinkled with the chilli.

SALMON & SWEETCORN CHOWDER

SERVES 2

200g drained, tinned potatoes, finely sliced

300ml chicken or fish stock

100g drained, tinned sweetcorn

75g salmon paste

2 tbsp milk (optional)

salt and pepper

This recipe is a simple but filling soup made from a small jar of cheap salmon paste, tinned potatoes and sweetcorn. It easily passes muster as fancy fare among my friends, for barely any effort at all. If you want to make it even more la-di-dah, stir in a few tablespoons of tinned spinach towards the end.

Pop the potatoes into a large saucepan. Add the stock, and bring to the boil. Reduce to a simmer for a minute.

Add the sweetcorn to the pan. Stir in the salmon paste. Cook for 15 minutes until everything is super soft. Add the milk to make it creamy, if you like, and season with salt and pepper, to taste.

You can serve it now, or blend half of it and return it all to the pot, for a thicker, creamier soup.

PASTA WITH COD ROE,
PEAS & LEMON

SERVES 2

salt and pepper

150g spaghetti

100g peas, tinned or frozen

a small knob of butter, or 2 tbsp oil

100g frozen sliced onion or 1 small onion, finely sliced

1 x 125g tin of cod roe in brine, drained

100ml cream (any kind) or cream cheese

a fistful of fresh chopped parsley, plus extra to serve

1 tbsp lemon juice

This recipe was inspired by Jocasta Innes' *The Pauper's Cookbook*, the definitive guide to cooking on a budget. Roe is inexpensive to buy in tins and, with its distinctive flavour, a little goes a long way.

Bring a pan of salted water to the boil, and add the spaghetti. Cook for 8–10 minutes. Add the peas for the last 2 minutes.

Meanwhile, heat the butter or oil in a frying pan, add the onion and cook over a low heat for 8–10 minutes until softened and translucent.

Tip the roe into a blender, with the cream or cheese, and the parsley. Season well and pulse until smooth. Add it to the pan with the onion and let it warm through over a low heat.

Drain and rinse the spaghetti and peas, then add them to the pan with the creamed roe. Toss everything together, then warm through. Serve with a generous dash of lemon juice, extra pepper and the remaining parsley.

SARDINE RILLETTES

SERVES 2

1 onion or 100g frozen sliced onion

2 x 90g tins of sardines in oil

a fistful of fresh flat-leaf parsley leaves, chopped (optional)

zest and juice of 1 lemon or 2 tbsp bottled lemon juice

salt and pepper

It's pronounced 'ree-yet' and until I'd heard it said out loud, I merrily called it 'rill-etts' in my coarse Essex accent, and even when corrected in polite company, I didn't care. It's a coarse and chunky pâté, usually made from pork or rabbit, but I like this simple sardine version.

Very finely dice the onion, then dice it some more, then dice it again. You want it minced, virtually undetectable, in teeny tiny pieces.

Remove the sardines from the tins, keeping the oil. Carefully open each one down the back and belly with a small sharp knife, then remove the backbone and any large visible bones. Discard the bones, and put the sardines into a bowl.

Mash the sardines with a fork, then add the onion and parsley. Grate over the lemon zest, if using, squeeze in the juice, and mix well with a fork to form a rough paste.

Season to taste. It can be served immediately, or chilled and brought to near room temperature to serve. I like mine spread on hot toast, then dunked in tomato soup for a quick, lazy dinner.

SMOKEY ROES ONE-POT DINNER

SERVES 2

500g drained, tinned potatoes, cut in half

2 tbsp oil

generous shake of paprika

salt and pepper

100g frozen sliced onion or 1 small onion, finely sliced

100g drained cod or herring roe

100g green beans or spinach, fresh or tinned

1 tbsp lemon juice

A tin of potatoes, a tin of cod or herring roe, and some fresh or tinned spinach or green beans make for a surprisingly easy and delicious dinner.

Toss the potatoes into a large, shallow frying pan along with the oil, paprika and salt and pepper. Add the onion and cook on a high heat for 5 minutes, then reduce the heat to medium and cook for 10 minutes more, until the onion is softened and the potatoes are crisp at the edges.

Stir through the roe, along with the green beans or spinach. Dress with lemon juice. Turn the heat up high again to blast it all, and serve warm or cold.

MEATS

CORNED BEEF BOLOGNESE

700g corned beef
(approx 2 tins), cut
into 1cm slices

1 x 500g carton of
passata or 1 x 400g
tin of chopped
tomatoes

1 tbsp garlic paste, or
2 cloves of garlic,
finely chopped

1 tsp dried herbs
(mixed, or rosemary,
thyme or oregano all
work)

salt and pepper

1 tsp lemon juice

300g dried spaghetti
or other long pasta

cheese, to serve

Corned beef was a staple of my childhood, often eaten on white toast with brown sauce, hot enough that the meagre slice of corned beef would melt disconcertingly into the toast. I first made this recipe for a foodbank in Birmingham, as part of a set of recipes that could be made from foodbank boxes. I have jazzed it up a little with a bit of garlic, but it remains an easy staple to throw together in a hurry. If you want to bulk it out to make it go further, you can add a tin or two of brown or green lentils, or some mushrooms; both work pretty well!

Pop your corned beef slices into a large saucepan along with the passata or chopped tomatoes. Put the pan over a medium heat, and add the garlic, herbs and a pinch of salt.

Cook for around 10 minutes – the beef should start to fall apart in the pan. You may need to give it a hand by breaking it up with a fork or a masher, or just give it a good stir with a wooden spoon. Turn the heat down low, add the lemon juice and some pepper, and cook for a further 15 minutes; the timing is key to develop the flavour as the tomatoes reduce slightly, concentrating into a thick, unctuous, meaty sauce.

Bring a separate pan of water to the boil and pop in your pasta. Turn the heat down to a simmer (small bubbles, not too explosive) and cook for 8–10 minutes until the pasta is soft. Remove from the heat and set it to one side while the Bolognese finishes cooking. You can leave the pasta in its cooking water for a few minutes so it doesn't go cold, but any longer than that and it will start to go a bit gloopy around the edges.

When the Bolognese is cooked to your liking (taste it and find out), remove it from the heat. Drain the pasta and serve it with the Bolognese dolloped on top. Grate the cheese over, if using, and enjoy.

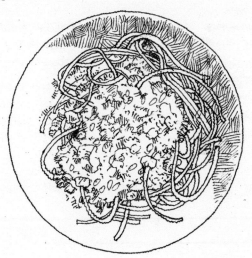

BEEFYBOOZY

SERVES 4–6

1 x 400g tin of
carrots, drained and
rinsed

250ml wine or cider

100g frozen sliced
onion or 1 small
onion, finely sliced

2 tbsp garlic paste or
6 fat cloves of garlic,
crushed

1 x 400g tin of brown
lentils, drained and
rinsed

1 tsp dried mixed
herbs

350ml chicken, beef
or vegetable stock

1 x 400g tin of stewed
steak

1 tbsp tomato purée
or ketchup

pepper

This is based on a recipe I make a lot at home made with just lentils; it's a hearty, filling stew of puréed carrots, salty stock, rich fragrant herbs and whatever dregs of wine, beer or cider I have to hand. For this book I added a can of stewed steak, carefully rinsed of all the claggy nasty gravy it comes submerged in, and gifted it to a friend and her husband to taste-test for me. The method may seem a tad precocious, but the results were met with boundless enthusiasm, so it's certainly worth it. The smooth sauce base, with the soft swollen lentils and falling-apart beef makes this perfect comforting nursery food, an excellent pie filling or base for a mash-topped cottage-pie-type thing, as well as a standalone hearty casserole. The name comes from me impotently attempting to describe it to a colleague as 'a kind of beefy … boozy … beefyboozy.' And it stuck.

First make the sauce base, and bear with me here as this method may seem a little bizarre, but it works wonderfully.

Tip the carrots into a small blender. Add the wine or cider, onion and garlic, and blend until smooth. Tip it into a large saucepan.

Add the lentils and herbs to the pan and set it over a medium heat. Cook for 30 minutes, gradually adding the stock and stirring, until the lentils are soft but still holding their shape.

Tip the pieces of stewed steak into a colander or sieve and thoroughly rinse them under a cold tap for a few seconds, shaking vigorously to loosen the gravy. You might want to send a slug of very hot water down your sink afterwards to flush it away, too. Tip the steak into the pan and cook for a further 10 minutes to warm it through and really soften it up so it's nice and tender.

Stir through the purée or ketchup, finish with a little black pepper, and serve.

CORNED BEEF CHILLI

SERVES 6–8, GENEROUSLY

1 small onion, diced, or 100g sliced frozen onions

6 fat cloves of garlic, crushed, or 3 tbsp garlic paste

2 tbsp oil

350g corned beef (around 1 large tin)

1 x 400g tin of kidney beans

1 x 400g tin of any other beans

2 x 400g tins of chopped tomatoes

2 tbsp paprika, sweet or smoked

2 tbsp ground cumin

salt and pepper

200ml red wine or strong black tea (optional)

20g dark chocolate (optional)

I made this recipe as part of a pop-up restaurant with an energy company and a food charity. The project demonstrated what could be cooked from tins to unsuspecting diners and had a serious message around the choice many people up and down the UK, and across the world, face in choosing between eating and heating. The corned beef disappears into the chilli, providing a salty, meaty background taste to the beans, so use denser beans that will hold their own; kidney, brown lentils and black eyed beans are good or black beans and adzuki if you can find them.

Sling the onion and garlic in a large pan. Add the oil.

Carefully remove the corned beef from the can and dice it into small pieces, less than 1cm each. Add to the pan. Drain and rinse the beans and add those too. Pour over the tomatoes, and add the paprika, cumin, salt and pepper, and bring to a medium heat.

Cook, stirring, for 7–8 minutes, then reduce the heat. Add the wine (or tea!), and the chocolate, if using, and continue cooking for 16–18 minutes, until glossy and dark and smelling fantastic.

Bring to a high heat to serve, and enjoy with rice, or whatever you like. This also freezes very well.

HOT OR COLD
CORONATION CHICKEN

SERVES 2

1 x 400g tin of
chicken in white
sauce

1 tbsp mayonnaise

1 tbsp mango
chutney

2 tbsp raisins or
sultanas

1 tbsp curry powder,
mild or medium

This dish has somewhat fallen out of favour of late.
Coronation chicken is, however, a classic, and works well
cold in sandwiches or pitta breads, warm in toasties with
lashings of cheese, and piping hot dolloped on rice or
over buttery jacket potatoes.

Spoon the chicken into a medium saucepan and carefully scrape
off as much of the white sauce as you can, leaving a little intact.
Keep it if you can think of a use for it – the most frugal among
you may retain it as some kind of soup thickener, but I have to
admit even I have my limits as to what I will hoard in my fridge.
Bring it to a medium heat and break up the chicken with a
wooden spoon until it is tender and in tiny pieces.

Stir through the mayo, mango chutney, raisins or sultanas and
curry powder, and warm through gently until piping hot.

Serve immediately, or, if you prefer to serve cold, allow to cool
and transfer to a sealed container in the fridge. It will keep for
up to 3 days.

TENDER-SPICED CHICKEN WITH OLIVES & MANDARINS

SERVES 6-8 GENEROUSLY

200g drained, tinned mandarins

1 x 400g tin of brown or green lentils, drained and rinsed

1 x 400g tin of chopped tomatoes

400g drained, tinned spinach, or frozen spinach

12 black or green olives, pitted

2 tbsp garlic paste, or 4 fat cloves of garlic, crushed

1 stock cube, vegetable or chicken

salt and pepper

1 tbsp ground cumin

➜

This simple recipe calls on a rich, complex layer of flavours to deliver a sweet, spicy and ultimately very healthy dinner. Enjoy it as a stew, or as a pie filling, or in puff pastry as hot-or-cold pasties. It freezes well, too.

First make the base for your stew; add the mandarins, lentils, tomatoes, spinach, olives and garlic to a large pan. Crumble in the stock cube and add 400ml water. Season with a little salt and pepper. Bring to the boil, then reduce to a simmer. Add the spices, then cook for 40 minutes over a medium heat.

Thoroughly rinse the chicken of all the white sauce – it is not required in this recipe and will only serve to dampen the flavour. (Although if you would prefer a creamier base, I suppose you could add it and double the spices to bring the flavour back, but I haven't tried it myself!)

1 tsp ground
turmeric

1 tsp paprika

1 x 400g tin of
chicken in white
sauce

1 tsp dried oregano
or other dried herbs

splash of lemon
juice, to serve

a pinch of dried chilli
flakes, to serve

Add the chicken – with or without the sauce – and the herbs to the pan. Cook for a further 20 minutes, stirring well to break the chicken up into smaller pieces; this makes it go further and taste more tender.

Add a dash of lemon juice and chilli flakes to serve.

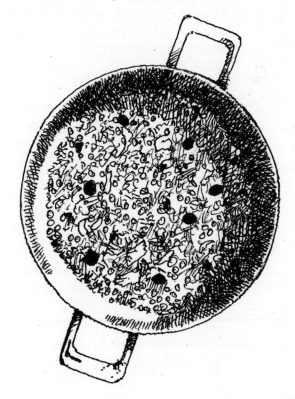

HARIRA

SERVES 4

1 x 400g tin of stewed steak

1 x 400g tin of green or brown lentils, drained and rinsed

1 x 400g tin of chickpeas, drained and rinsed

100g frozen sliced onion or 1 small onion, finely sliced

1 x 400g tin of chopped tomatoes

1 tbsp plain flour

salt

½ tsp black pepper, plus extra to serve

1 tsp ground turmeric

½ tsp ground cinnamon

1 tsp grated fresh root ginger

1 tbsp lemon juice

Harira is a popular Middle Eastern soup, and, like many recipes, there are as many variations as there are individual families throughout the world! Key base ingredients include lentils or chickpeas, a small amount of meat, onions, rice and herbs and spices, including saffron or turmeric, ginger and pepper for heat. Traditional recipes use dried pulses, left to soak and then cooked for hours on a gentle heat; but this tinned recipe, while not strictly authentic, is quicker and simpler to make.

Drain and rinse the stewed steak – it feels a little odd the first time you do this, but you really don't want all that sticky gravy in your harira. So tip it into a sieve or colander and run it under a cold tap, shaking gently to make sure you get it all off. (It does seem a tad wasteful, but I've racked my brain and can't think of any use for it – if you come up with one, do write and let me know!) When thoroughly rinsed, set it to one side.

Tip the lentils and chickpeas into a large saucepan, add the onion and tomatoes and flour, and cover with 600ml water. Bring to the boil, then reduce to a simmer. When simmering, add a pinch of the salt, the black pepper, spices, ginger and the steak. Cook for 1 hour on a low heat to allow the pulses to really soften and the soup to thicken.

Finish with the lemon juice and a little extra pepper, and serve.

PORK, PEAR & STUFFING LOAF

SERVES 6-8

1 x 340g tin of Spam or other tinned ham

1 x 410g tin of pears, drained

80g sage and onion stuffing mix

salt and pepper

oil, for greasing

When I was first developing this recipe, I started off by slinging a tin of Spam in a blender, partly out of mischief, partly to create 'spreadable Spam', and partly to test my own stomach lining as the stench of reprocessed processed meat permeated my tiny kitchen. It was not, dear reader, a pleasant experience, but it was, admittedly, a fun one. I scraped the meat into a bowl, added some grated tinned pear and some stuffing mix, and this was the result. And it is absolutely delicious.

Preheat the oven to 180°C (fan 160°C/350°F/gas 4).

First grate your Spam. It's not the greatest job in the world, but just get on with it. Then grate your pears, which will be slippery blighters, so hold them tightly. Put both into a large mixing bowl, then add your stuffing mix. Season with a little salt and pepper, and stir well to combine.

Spoon the mixture into an oiled 450g loaf tin or small, deep, ovenproof tray. Bake in the centre of the oven for 30 minutes, until firm and a knife inserted into the centre comes out clean. If the top starts to brown too much before the middle is cooked, cover it with foil or baking parchment and return it to the oven to continue to cook.

TIP

Try this on its own as a way of stretching a meat course, or stuff it up the bum of a chicken heading into the oven to roast.

DOG IN A HOLE

30g butter or
2 tbsp cooking oil

1 x 400g tin of hot
dog sausages,
drained

100g plain flour

salt

1 egg

300ml milk

My nine-year-old son loves this version of toad in the hole – and at the end of a long working week, I'm very thankful for that! If I'm feeling like a nod to virtue, I empty a can of carrots and a can of beans into the mixture for two kinds of vegetables, but sometimes, goodness, who cares?

Preheat the oven to 200°C (fan 180°C/400°F/gas 6).

First grab a roasting dish, around 25 x 30cm, or a deep round cake tin of about the same size will do the job.

Pop the butter or oil and sausages, into the tin. Cook for around 5 minutes, giving the tin a jostle halfway through to make sure they warm evenly.

While the sausages are warming, get a mixing bowl. Add the flour, a pinch of salt and the egg, and half the milk. Beat them together to form a smooth batter. Pour in the rest of the milk and continue to beat until very smooth.

Remove the roasting tin from the oven and pour the batter in. Move the sausages so they are roughly evenly distributed. Bake for 40 minutes until the batter is risen and golden. DO NOT OPEN THE OVEN DOOR until the 40 minutes are over else your batter will deflate! Serve immediately.

TIN CAN COOK

CHICKEN & MUSHROOM CURRY

SERVES 4

1 x 400g tin of chicken in white sauce

1 x 290g tin of mushrooms, button or sliced, drained

1 tbsp curry powder

1 tbsp cooking oil or 15g butter

salt and pepper

a dash of lemon juice

There is a certain amount of sniffiness around premixed curry powders, but there needn't be; they are simply a mix of garam masala and turmeric, and usually cheaper than buying them individually. Supermarket own-brand curry powder is one of my store-cupboard staples, used for pepping up potatoes and eggs, and here for transforming a tasteless tin into a warm, spicy and delicious meal in minutes. For a nod to authenticity, you could add 200g chopped onion, fresh or frozen, but it isn't essential.

In my other books I have many long, slow, multi-spiced, more traditional curries, but this is a handy one to have on standby when the takeaway beckons. You can replace the mushrooms with lentils, peas, or any other vegetable you like or happen to have in.

Tip the chicken into a saucepan over a medium heat. Add the mushrooms too. Spoon in the curry powder, oil or butter, and a little salt and pepper, and add a splash of water to loosen it.

Cook for 15 minutes, breaking the chicken up with a spoon – this makes it taste more tender and gives the illusion of more chicken in your curry than there actually is, helping it go further!

Season to taste with pepper, if needed, and lemon juice, and serve.

CHICKEN, HAM & MUSHROOMS IN A FANCY HAT

SERVES 6

1 x 400g tin of chicken in white sauce

1 x 340g tin of Spam or other tinned ham

100g tinned spinach

1 x 400g tin of mushroom soup

salt and pepper

200g filo pastry, or ready-rolled puff or shortcrust pastry

oil, for brushing

I am a real traditionalist when it comes to pies being pies – that is, having a floor, walls and a ceiling. You wouldn't call a hat a home, and in the same manner, a casserole in a hat is not a pie. The worst offender I ever had was at a pub in Lancashire, where, to be honest, I expected better. I was served a few floating cobbles of pastry in a stew that they had dared to advertise as a pie. I was astonished at their barefaced effrontery. And so this lazy dinner is absolutely not a pie. It's a casserole with a fancy hat. My friend Caroline, who has faithfully tasted almost every recipe in this book, described this as 'gastropub good'. Which, given its origins, made me very happy.

Preheat the oven to 170°C (fan 150°C/325°F/gas 3).

Tip the chicken in white sauce into a large pan. Prise the Spam from its tin and cut into small cubes, around 1cm, and add those to the pan. Drain the spinach, if necessary, and spoon it in, followed with the mushroom soup. Turn the heat to medium and cook for 5 minutes just to warm everything through and combine it, breaking the chicken up with your wooden spoon as it heats through. Season with salt and a little pepper.

Spoon the pie filling into a deep dish or cake tin – mine was 20cm square. Top with the pastry and brush the top with oil. Bake in the centre of the oven for 30 minutes, or until the pastry is golden. Serve hot or cold.

TIP
I used shop-bought filo, because I like it, and it can be bought relatively cheaply in the freezer department and defrosted overnight in the fridge, but shortcrust or puff pastry would work too, and the same rules apply.

SWEET & SOUR PICKIN' BALLS

MAKES 20ISH

1 x 340g tin of Spam or other tinned ham

1 x 400g tin of chicken in white sauce, rinsed and finely chopped

2 slices bread, grated or blitzed in a blender (optional)

salt

2 pinches of Chinese 5 spice (optional)

1 x 200g tin of pineapple, drained

1 x 400g tin of chopped tomatoes

2 tbsp tomato purée or ketchup

1 tbsp vinegar

flour, for dusting

These were originally made for my then-eight-year-old son, after he asked me for sweet and sour chicken balls and I decided to see if I could mix chicken and pork together in some sort of grotesque experiment to give him the familiar taste of our local takeaway, but from tins. To cut a long story short, these are probably ideally suited for the less-discerning palate of children, although my more grown-up friends enjoyed them lightly battered and deep-fried, but I think that says a lot about the company I keep rather than the recipe itself.

Open the Spam and finely mince it – you might find this easier to do with a grater. Pop the pork and chicken in a mixing bowl and combine, adding the breadcrumbs to hold them together, if required. Add a pinch of salt and a pinch of Chinese 5 spice, if using, to give it some life. Pop in the fridge for 30 minutes to chill and firm.

Meanwhile, make the sweet and sour sauce. You can blend it for a smooth, sticky, glossy sauce, or leave it whole, depending if you have a blender and what your personal preferences are. If blending, blend the drained pineapple and whole can of tomatoes together, then pour into a saucepan. If you aren't blending them, just tip them both into a pan, holding back the pineapple juice to use another time. Add some salt, a pinch of Chinese 5 spice, purée and the vinegar. Bring to the boil, then reduce to a simmer for 20 minutes, or until thick and glossy.

Preheat the oven to 180°C (fan 160°C/350°F/gas 4).

Form the chilled meat mixture into walnut-sized balls. Roll them in a little flour, and place on a baking tray. Bake in the centre of the oven for 25 minutes, turning over halfway through to cook evenly.

When the balls are cooked, pour over the hot sauce, and serve.

THREE-TIN TENDER (BEEF IN SORT-OF BARBECUE SAUCE)

SERVES 1–2, DEPENDING ON APPETITE

1 x 400g tin of chopped tomatoes

330ml full-sugar cola

1 x 400g tin of stewed steak

Describing this as barbecue anything feels wildly disingenuous, not least because it hasn't been anywhere near a barbecue, so the familiar, sweet-sticky BBQ-style sauce is where this gets its name. The quantities given here will serve one or two people, depending on appetite, and can be easily scaled up to serve more, though it will need a longer cooking time. To make it go further, pack the sauce out with onions (100g per person) or kidney beans (1 tin per same-sized tin of steak).

You can make this fancy by adding paprika or mustard for heat, or a dash of vinegar to offset the sweetness, but it works perfectly well just as it is. A large pot of this makes an excellent dinner, served atop a pile of mash. I use cheap full-sugar cola in mine, because I care not for preachery, but the diet version works as well.

First pour the tomatoes and cola into a large pan. Bring slowly to the boil, keeping an eye on it and stirring well, as the bubbles in the cola will rise rapidly and boil over if you don't keep them under control. When it starts to come to a boil, reduce to a simmer and cook for 20 minutes to reduce and thicken the sauce.

Tip the stewed steak into a sieve or colander and rinse off the gravy as best you can, then add the meat to the pot. Turn the heat back up. Cook for a further 10 minutes, or as long as you can spare – the longer this cooks for, the thicker and glossier the sauce becomes, but 10 minutes will suffice.

A simple trick for thickening a sauce without using too much heat is to allow it to cool completely, as the cooling action thickens the sauce (because, science) and the pot will continue to slowly cook everything as it cools. Simply heat through when required, and serve.

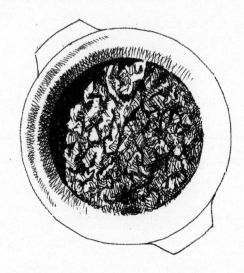

MINCE & ONIONS WITH NOTIONS

SERVES 4

2 x 398g tins of minced beef and onions in gravy

100g frozen sliced onions or 1 small onion, finely chopped

100ml red wine

1 tsp mixed dried herbs

1 tbsp tomato purée or ketchup

toast, to serve (optional)

'Notions' is what my Northern Irish Granny Beatty would have called 'ideas about yourself', or popping your head a little above your station. This mince and onions dish certainly has notions of its own, transformed from slop in a tin to a rich and delicious dinner, ideal served on a pile of buttery mashed potatoes or, for even more excitement, creamy peachy-coloured carrot and potato mash. Of course, you could make this with fresh mince and onions very easily, by browning the mince and onions in a pan, adding gravy and wine, but this version is deliberately simple, and deliciously so. It makes for an excellent filling for a pasty, if you're inclined that way. To make it go even further, and more nutritious, add a can of drained green or brown lentils too.

Pour the mince and onions into a medium saucepan. Add the onion, red wine, herbs and purée.

Cook on a low heat for 20 minutes until the sauce has reduced and it suddenly smells like something you want to eat, rather than whatever just slopped out of the tin. Serve with toast.

TIP
I serve mine on toast, because toast is fantastic and an oft-underrated vessel for a quick and easy dinner. To impress a friend – said with my tongue wedged firmly in my cheek – place a smattering of spinach or salad between the toast and the mince and onions, and grated cheese on top. It's quick, it's simple, it doesn't really count as cooking, but it's a fantastic little dinner for when you don't feel like stretching yourself.

CHICKEN, LENTIL & LIME PICKLE CURRY

SERVES 2, GENEROUSLY

1 x 400g tin of chicken in sauce

1 x 400g tin of coconut milk

1 tbsp curry powder, mild or medium

1 x 400g tin of brown or green lentils, drained and rinsed

100g peanut butter, smooth or crunchy

3 tbsp lime pickle

This curry was an accidental tinkering with a couple of tins to feed friends for lunch. Vegetarian and vegan readers can omit the chicken and replace it with spinach for a different – but just as delicious – idea. It's sweet, sour, tangy, spicy and very very moreish.

First rinse the chicken of any sauce that it has come in, unless it is a chicken in curry sauce, in which case omit the curry powder from the ingredients list and just sling the whole lot into a pan. Pour over the coconut milk and bring to a medium heat, stirring well to combine. Add the curry powder, if using. Add the lentils to the pan. Stir in the peanut butter and lime pickle.

Cook for 20 minutes, breaking up the chicken with a fork or spoon into small pieces. Remove from the heat and serve.

SOMETHING LIKE A FEIJOADA

SERVES 4

1 x 400g tin of black beans, drained and rinsed

100g frozen sliced onion or 1 small onion, finely sliced

2 tbsp garlic paste or 4 fat cloves of garlic, crushed

2 tbsp tomato purée or ketchup

1 tbsp paprika

1 chicken or beef stock cube

1 x 300g tin of mandarins, drained

1 x 400g tin of stewed steak, drained and rinsed

a few pinches of dried chilli flakes

Feijoada is a Brazilian stew, traditionally made with pork, beef and black beans. Some versions are served with caramelized orange slices on top and stirred through, so I have used mandarins here; their bright citrus flavour helps to lift the heady, heavy black beans and beef. This may sound an odd combination but it is truly delicious. My apologies to my Brazilian friends – if you do get the chance to make an authentic feijoada, seize it, it knocks absolute spots off this one, but I've done the best I could with what I had!

This improves with a day's rest, as do most of us, so keep leftovers in a sealed container in the fridge and enjoy them the next day.

Tip the black beans into a large saucepan. Add the onion, garlic, tomato purée and paprika. Cover with 700ml water and crumble in the stock cube, then bring to the boil. Reduce to a simmer and cook for 30 minutes, until the beans have started to soften.

Add the mandarins and stewed steak to the pot. Cook for a further 20 minutes, then finish with dried chilli flakes to taste, and serve.

PUDDINGS

FRUIT COCKTAIL CAKE

SERVES 8

250g butter, plus extra to grease the cake tin

200g caster or granulated sugar

3 eggs

200g tin of fruit cocktail, drained

200g self-raising flour

This bejewelled jolly little number is a simple way to use up any kind of tinned fruit; I like the veritable party that a fruit cocktail brings to the table – and the inevitable hunt for the scant cherry half that there only ever seems to be one of!

Preheat the oven to 180°C (fan 160°C/350°F/gas 4) and lightly grease a 20cm round or square cake tin.

Beat the butter and sugar together in a mixing bowl with a fork or wooden spoon until well combined. Break in the eggs and mix together, beating until smooth.

Add the fruit cocktail to the mixing bowl and stir through quickly. Add the flour, and mix well to combine into a soft, sweet batter.

Pour the batter into the tin and bake in the centre of the oven for around 45 minutes – depending on the size of your tin. A shallow tin will cook faster, whereas a deeper tin will take its time. To check if it is cooked through, insert a sharp knife into the centre of the cake. If the knife comes out clean, the cake is ready. Allow to cool in the tin for 10 minutes before turning out and slicing.

The cake can be enjoyed hot or cold. Leftovers freeze well for up to 3 months, wrapped in foil or popped in a freezer bag.

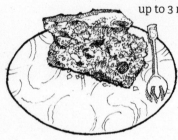

TIN CAN COOK

RHUBARB & CUSTARD CRUMBLE

SERVES 6

2 x 500g tins of
rhubarb, drained

2 x 400g tins of
custard

200g plain flour

100g cold butter

100g oats

50g sugar (the
custard is pretty
sweet so the topping
doesn't have to be)

This is very simple to make and even simpler to eat.
In my household, custard is served with crumble, no
questions asked. I generally shudder at warm custard –
I know some of you may disagree, but it's a very personal
thing – but will happily accept it in this form! If you
aren't a rhubarb fan, tinned apple works well here too.

Preheat your oven to 180°C (fan 160°C/350°F/gas 4).

Tip the rhubarb into the bottom of an ovenproof dish.
Pour the custard on top.

In a large mixing bowl, make the crumble topping. Tip in
the flour, then add the butter in little pieces. Rub the butter
between your fingers with the flour until the mixture resembles
breadcrumbs. Stir in the oats and sugar to combine.

Spoon the crumble topping onto the rhubarb and custard.
Bake in the centre of the oven for 40 minutes, or until the
topping is golden. Serve hot or cold.

PBJ CRUMBLE

SERVES 8-10

2 x 400g tins of berries and cherries

100g strawberry jam

100g butter or alternative

100g peanut butter, crunchy or smooth

50g sugar (you can increase or decrease this according to taste)

200g plain flour

I am near fanatical about peanut butter and jam – or peanut butter and jelly, for my readers across the pond. I have previously made PBJ cookies, PBJ microwave brownies for BBC *Good Food*, a PBJ semifreddo ice cream for a Small Boy and a PBJ pie with peanut butter hand-kneaded into the pastry, stuffed with thick, unctuous strawberry jam. My latest homage to my favourite marriage of flavours is this – the PBJ crumble I served at a lunch for ten, which was met with a chorus of rapture as I placed it on the table (readers who are old enough – or young enough – to have seen the original *Toy Story* film, it was like offering it to a crowd of small green aliens …).

It went down a treat with all ten of us, even the unenthusiastic crumble hater and the one who insisted she didn't like peanut butter – and four of us had generous seconds (and six were mildly disappointed). It can be made gluten free, either by swapping the flour for your preferred gluten-free brand, or by blitzing oats in a blender or food processor to a powdery consistency, and using those instead. The gluten-free options would make for a drier crumble topping, but the base is sufficiently sloppy to compensate.

First, grab a nice deep ovenproof dish to cook it in, and turn your oven on to 180°C (fan 160°C/350°F/gas 4) if you are planning to cook this straight away. If not, you can keep it chilled and cook it later on.

Tip the berries into the bottom of the dish and gently shake them to evenly coat the base. Dot in the jam – approximately 8 tablespoons – at roughly even locations around the berries. It will melt nicely when it starts to cook!

Now make the crumble topping. Put the butter and peanut butter into a mixing bowl and cream together with a fork until well combined. Add the sugar and cream together again. Add the flour and rub the mixture between your fingertips until it looks like large breadcrumbs. Spread this evenly on top of the berries and jam.

When you are ready to cook, pop it into the oven for 30 minutes until the berries are cooked and bubbling and the crumble topping is golden.

TINNED CHERRY CHOCOLATE FUDGE

MAKES A LOT OF FUDGE

400g dark chocolate

100g caster or icing sugar

200g tinned cherries

25g butter

1 x 400g tin of condensed milk

You can make this recipe with or without tinned cherries, depending on whether you have them, or your personal preference – a dollop of red jam does the same job at a pinch. I have made variations of this fudge with apple filling, cinnamon and white chocolate, drained and pressed mandarins and milk chocolate to emulate a certain Christmas orange, but this one is my favourite by far. It tastes luxuriously sumptuous, and we all need a bit of that from time to time.

Lightly grease a baking tin, mine was 20cm square, but any size will do.

Break up the dark chocolate into a large microwave-proof bowl, then add the sugar and set to one side for a moment.

Pop a sieve over a medium saucepan, and drain the cherries, so the juice is caught in the pan. (Keep it for the cherry cordial recipe on page 149!)

Using a fork or spoon, mash the cherries against the sieve for 5 vigorous minutes to squeeze out as much of the juice as possible; as I said to my son who gleefully undertook this repetitive task, 'if the cherries are too wet, the fudge won't set!'. When you are satisfied that they have been squished to oblivion, set them to one side and return your attention to the chocolate bowl.

Pop the bowl of chocolate and sugar in the microwave on a medium setting – too high and it will burn the chocolate – and microwave for 9 seconds to start to melt the chocolate. Remove from the microwave, stir, and repeat. Add the butter and return to the microwave one more time for another 9 seconds, until the chocolate is liquid and glossy. Stir to combine.

Tip the cherries into the chocolate and pour in the condensed milk, scraping it all from the edges of the tin. Stir through, mixing well to combine the ingredients. Pour into the lightly greased tin and chill in the fridge for 2 hours until set. Cut into small pieces and enjoy. The fudge will need to be stored in the fridge, and will keep for 2 weeks.

CHOCOLATE PEAR CAKE
VE

SERVES 6

75g applesauce from a jar

75ml oil, plus extra for greasing

75g sugar

1 x 400g tin of pears

175ml coconut milk or other plant-based milk

175g self-raising flour

1 tsp bicarbonate of soda

1 tbsp ground ginger or cinnamon

6 tbsp cocoa powder

This soft, sweet, rich and heavy cake was made just for this book, as I sat surveying tins of fruit and wondering how to plump up my pudding chapter. My eyes roved greedily over the tinned peaches, pears and cherries, looking for inspiration, and there it was. Fat, fulsome pears swimming sodden in their own slippery, succulent syrup. I licked my lips. I'm licking them now, typing up the recipe, my meagre home rich with the scent of freshly baked goods, impatiently picking at the slice I have promised myself as a reward for committing it to paper. I love this, and it's all the better for using tinned pears; I hope you love it too.

Spoon the applesauce into a large mixing bowl and add the oil and sugar. Mix well with a fork or wooden spoon until well combined.

Drain the pears and reserve the juice – I pour mine straight into a glass, dilute with water and drink it. Delicious! Pop the pears into a small blender, if you have one, and blend until smooth. If you don't have a blender, finely slice them by hand. You'll get a different cake, but still a very delicious one. Either way, blended or sliced, pop the pears into the mixing bowl with the applesauce-sugar-oil mix and stir well. Add the coconut milk and mix well.

Add in the flour, bicarbonate of soda, ginger or cinnamon and cocoa, and stir well to form a smooth, glossy cake batter.

Turn on the oven to 180°C (fan 160°C/350°F/gas 4). Lightly grease a 450g loaf tin and pour in the mixture. Bake in the centre of the oven for 45 minutes, until risen and a small sharp knife inserted into the centre comes out clean. Remove from the oven but leave in the tin for 20 minutes to cool and firm up, before turning out and serving.

CHERRY BATTER PUDDING

SERVES 4

100g plain flour

300ml milk

1 large egg

400g tin of cherries

50g sugar, if making
a syrup (optional)

butter, for greasing

This is a cheaper take on a clafoutis, and a less stressful one, too. It's not cloyingly sweet, so dredge it with a little sugar before serving. And serve swiftly; it starts to deflate after a little while, making your centrepiece a little less spectacular than it could be!

First grab a large mixing bowl and beat together the flour, milk and egg to form a batter. Pop it in the fridge for an hour to chill; the best batters are those that go into a hot oven from a cold fridge, it's science, and it's almost foolproof.

When the batter is chilled, drain the cherries. I reserve the juice and either drink it as a cordial (see opposite), or make it into a syrup by warming it with 50g sugar for 10 minutes and reducing it down to something sticky to pour over my pud.

Lightly grease a cake tin or small roasting dish with butter. Preheat the oven to 200°C (fan 180°C/400°F/gas 6) for 10 minutes – one of the very rare times I will recommend a preheat! Gently stir the cherries into the cold batter and pour into the tin. Bake on the middle shelf for 40 minutes, or until risen and golden. Serve immediately (with the syrup, if you've made it) or risk a flaccid pudding.

BONUS CHERRY CORDIAL
VE

SERVES A FEW

400ml leftover
tinned cherry juice

100g sugar

I came up with this after making the cherry chocolate fudge (see pages 144–5), and ended up with a pan of leftover juice from the tinned cherries. You can apply this method to any leftover tinned juice; I've done it with pear, pineapple and mandarin juice, too. Simply adjust the quantities according to how much juice you have, and make sure you store it in the fridge once cooled. The ratio I use is 1g of sugar per 4ml of juice, but you may wish to adjust this to taste.

Pour the cherry juice into a saucepan and add the sugar. Bring to the boil, then reduce to a simmer, stirring to dissolve the sugar.

Simmer for 10 minutes, then allow to cool completely. Pour into a sterilized jar or bottle (see method for doing this on page 58) and store in the fridge for up to 4 weeks. Serve generously diluted to taste with cold water.

FIVE-INGREDIENT STICKY TOFFEE PUDDING

SERVES 6

butter, for greasing

180g drained, tinned prunes (pitted are best for ease but if you can't find them, simply slip the stones out of each prune and discard)

2 eggs

1 x 400g tin of Carnation Caramel (or condensed milk if you can't find it)

180g self-raising flour

1 tsp bicarbonate of soda or 3 tsp baking powder

This segues away from a traditional toffee pudding with the use of prunes in place of dates, but the result is still sticky, sweet and caramelly comfort. Bliss. You'll notice there is no added butter or sugar in this recipe, which isn't an error; the condensed milk or caramel does the same job here. It does make for a lighter cake than the traditionally heavier sticky toffee pudding, so if you want to, you can add 50g melted butter or 50ml light cooking oil at the same time as the eggs.

Preheat your oven to 180°C (fan 160°C/350°F/gas 4) and lightly grease a 450g loaf or 20cm cake tin, or around six to eight small individual pudding moulds.

Next, drain the prunes and reserve the juice – I keep it diluted in a jar in the fridge to help relieve my young son when he is, shall we delicately say, a little bunged up in the middle. It can also be used to make a salad dressing or to add sweetness to a curry or chilli.

Tip the prunes into a mixing bowl and mash well with a fork or the side of a teaspoon to form a rough paste. If you have a small blender, you can use it for this task; I do when I want it done in a hurry, but it isn't essential. Add the eggs and beat well, then pour in two-thirds of the caramel or condensed milk.

Measure 160ml cold water. Add it to the bowl, a splash at a time, mixing well to loosen the prune-egg-caramel gloop in the bowl, until it is all combined. The caramel takes a little encouragement to join the rest of it, but a good beating soon sorts it out.

Shake in the flour – sift it if you must, I never bother – and the bicarb or baking powder, and mix well to form a loose, even-coloured batter.

Spoon the mixture into your tin; I like to use a rubber spatula to scrape in every last drop. If using pudding moulds, divide the mixture evenly between them until they are two-thirds full.

Bake a single large pudding in the centre of the oven for 45 minutes until risen and a deep toffee colour. Individual pudding moulds will need around 20 minutes, depending on their capacity.

While the sponge is cooking, pour the remaining caramel or condensed milk into a small saucepan. Add a splash of water and heat it to make a runny, syrupy sauce. Stir well until smooth and set to one side; you will need this later.

Check that the pudding is cooked by inserting a small sharp knife into the centre of it. If it comes out clean, it's done. If it has traces (or more) of batter on it, it needs another 10 minutes or so.

Remove from the oven when cooked and leave in the tin for 20 minutes to cool. This is important, the cake needs to chill out a bit else it may crack clean in two. Still perfectly edible, but heartbreaking nonetheless.

Remove from the oven and make approximately 12 holes in the cake from top to bottom with a skewer, or 30 holes with a cocktail stick. If making in pudding moulds, you can get away with 4–6 holes in each. Carefully pour the caramel syrup on the top so it soaks into the holes. Once cooled, remove carefully from the tin or moulds, and serve. It's called sticky pudding for a reason. Enjoy!

INDEX

TIN CAN COOK

THANK YOU

For Jonny and Louisa, for all their love (boundless), cups of tea (three this year and counting) and clean plates (thousands).

Thank you to my publisher Carole Tonkinson at Bluebird for her dogged belief in this book, and editors Martha Burley, Hockley Raven Spare and Zainab Dawood. To Rosemary Scoular for her unending support and care, Aoife Rice and Natalia Lucas for keeping me organised, and Caroline for turning up every day, eating all my food, and being generally fantastic.
To Garry Lemon at the Trussell Trust for his tireless advocacy for foodbanks and against their root causes, and thank you to every single foodbank volunteer and staff member who work to keep desperately hungry people fed, all year round, especially those at the Storehouse in Southend who kept me alive when I was in my darkest times. I owe you my life, and that is a debt that can never be repaid, but I hope this book helps a little for you to continue your good, and sadly essential, work.

Illustrations in the book

All illustrations are by John Bulley and Hattie Mitchell apart from pages 2, 7, 27, 41, 57, 79, 87, 103, 115 and 139 which are from Andrew Barron / Thextension.

REFERENCES

Information quoted in the Cansplaining section has been taken from a variety of research sources, including SELF Nutrition Data, www.foodmatters.com, www.CheckYourFood.com, *Medical News Today*, *Healthline*, *Food Safety Magazine*, *The Journal of Nutrition*, The American Institute of Nutrition, The Wistar Institute of Anatomy and Biology, Michigan State University, *Journal of the Science of Food and Agriculture*, University of California, *The Telegraph*, *Guardian* and the National Health Service.

1 Joy C Rickman, Diane M Barrett and Christine M Bruhn (2007). Nutritional comparison of fresh, frozen and canned fruits and vegetables. Part 1. Vitamins C and B and phenolic compounds. *Journal of the Science of Food and Agriculture*, p.942.
2 Joanna Blythman (2012). *What To Eat* (Fourth Estate).
3 Texas A&M AgriLife Communications (2012). Peaches, plums, nectarines give obesity, diabetes slim chance. *ScienceDaily*. www.sciencedaily.com/releases/2012/06/120618132921.htm
4 Perdomo F1, Cabrera Fránquiz F, Cabrera J, Serra-Majem L (2012). Influence of cooking procedure on the bioavailability of lycopene in tomatoes. www.ncbi.nlm.nih.gov/pubmed/23478703
5 Carr, S. and Smith, J. (2017) *Advanced Human Nutrition and Metabolism*, Seventh Edition. Wadsworth Publishing.
6 World Health Organisation. www.who.int/elena/bbc/fruit_vegetables_ncds/en/
7 American Hearth Association. www.ahajournals.org/lookup/doi/10.1161/CIR.0000000000000574
8 British Heart Foundation. www.bhf.org.uk/informationsupport/support/healthy-living/healthy-eating/salt
9 National Health Service. www.nhs.uk/conditions/vitamins-and-minerals/vitamin-d/

First published 2019 by Bluebird
an imprint of Pan Macmillan
20 New Wharf Road, London N1 9RR

Associated companies throughout the world www.panmacmillan.com

ISBN 978-1-5290-1528-7

9 8 7 6 5 4 3 2 1

A CIP catalogue record for this book is available from the British Library.

Printed and bound by CPI Group (UK) Ltd, Croydon, CR0 4YY

Publisher Carole Tonkinson

Senior Editor Martha Burley

Senior Production Controller Sarah Badhan

Interior Design Andrew Barron / Thextension

Cover and Endpaper Design Mel Four

Cover Photography Patricia Niven

Visit www.panmacmillan.com to read more about all our books and to buy them. You will also find features, author interviews and news of any author events, and you can sign up for e-newsletters so that you're always first to hear about our new releases.